Care for the Mental and Spiritual Health of Black Men

Religion and Race

Series Editors
Monica R. Miller, Lehigh University
Anthony B. Pinn, Rice University

The local/global connections between religion and race are complex, interrelated, ever changing, and undeniable. Religion and Race bridges these multifaceted dimensions within a context of cultural complexity and increasing socio-political realities of identity and difference in a multi-disciplinary manner that offers a strong platform for scholars to examine the relationship between religion and race. This series is committed to a range of social science and humanities approaches, including media studies, cultural studies, and feminist and queer methods, and welcomes books from a variety of global and cultural contexts from the modern period to projects considering the dynamics of the "postmodern" context. While the series will privilege monographs, it will also consider exceptional edited volumes. Religion and Race seeks to impact historical and contemporary cultural and socio-political conversations through comparative scholarly examinations that tap the similarities and distinctions of race across geographies within the context of a variety of religious traditions and practices.

Titles in the Series

Care for the Mental and Spiritual Health of Black Men

Hope to Keep Going

Nicholas Grier

LEXINGTON BOOKS
Lanham • Boulder • New York • London

Published by Lexington Books
An imprint of The Rowman & Littlefield Publishing Group, Inc.
4501 Forbes Boulevard, Suite 200, Lanham, Maryland 20706
www.rowman.com

6 Tinworth Street, London SE11 5AL

British Library Cataloguing in Publication Information Available

Library of Congress Cataloging-in-Publication Data

Library of Congress Control Number: 2019950744
ISBN 978-1-4985-6712-1 (cloth : alk. paper)
ISBN 978-1-4985-6714-5 (paper : alk. paper)
ISBN 978-1-4985-6713-8 (electronic)

To my sisters and brothers in the global village.
May we all flourish.

Contents

Acknowledgments

I want to thank God, the Universe, the ancestors, and my family for their life-giving support. I could not have completed this project without such a supportive village.

Thank you, Claremont School of Theology (CST) family. President Jeffrey Kuan and Dean Sheryl Kujawa-Holbrook have been most supportive of my work and professional development. Thank you for your support of this project. My CST faculty colleagues, Monica Coleman, Duane Bidwell, Grace Kao, Najeeba Syeed, and Belva Brown Jordan, have been most amazing and tremendously supportive! They seamlessly and quickly provided helpful feedback in the final stages of preparing this book for production. Thank you for your remarkable and life-giving support. Philip Clayton also provided a space for dialogue in his home. I am most thankful for these conversations that helped refine my ideas. I cherish our friendship. I am also thankful for Jeongyun Hur and Jessica Chapman who served as my research assistants during the writing process. Ms. Hur (soon-to-be Dr. Hur) researched articles and completed the index for this book. Ms. Chapman (soon-to-be Dr. Chapman) read through a draft of this book and offered helpful feedback. I am also tremendously grateful for all of my students at Claremont School of Theology. You are a most amazing and diverse group of people who will transform the world! Your thoughtful reflections and feedback during our class discussions have fueled my life's work. Thank you! Wishing you all the best in your future endeavors.

I am thankful for colleagues in the field who read earlier drafts of the manuscript. Specifically, Carroll Watkins Ali, Lee Butler, Jr., Duane Bidwell, and Elizabeth Pierre provided helpful feedback.

I am also thankful for my cousin, Andre Dennis, for his creative flow with Coloring Mental Health Collective and for his feedback on marketing materials for this book.

I am grateful for The Center for Religion and Psychotherapy of Chicago (CRPC) who supported this project through a book support grant. Thank you! I must also thank The Forum for Theological Exploration (FTE) for supporting an earlier version of this work during my year as an FTE dissertation fellow. The supportive network of FTE continues to be life-giving.

Publishing this project with Lexington Press would not have been possible if it were not for Anthony Pinn and Monica Miller extending a book contract. I am thankful for Dr. Pinn's invitation to send my work his way. Thank you for your encouragement to share my work. Your work and support of my work have been life-giving.

I must thank the following editors: Thank you, Henry Carrigan, for looking over the project for style and accessibility. Thank you, Diane Capitani, for your copy-editing work. Thank you, Michael Gibson, for your gracious support of this project. Thank you, Mikayla Mislak, for pushing this project through to its completion.

Stephen Ray, Lallene Rector, Phillis Sheppard, Lee Butler, Jr., Celia Brickman, and Jeffery Tribble were helpful guides during the early stages of my intellectual development. Thank you for your generous presence in my life.

I am thankful for my immediate family: Grace Grier, Arthur Grier, Gabriel Grier, Stephen Grier, and Dawn Grier, I love you dearly. I want to also acknowledge my biological father, Jimmy Orange. Wishing blessings on your life. Thank you to my extended family. I am also thankful for friendships with Grant Crusor, Marquis Hare, Kenya Tuttle, and Christopher Hubbard. I am because we are.

Introduction

A Prelude to Keep Going

In the film *Stomp the Yard*, Black men chant the following words during a fraternity initiation ceremony: "We got to keep pushing. We got to keep moving. We got to keep fighting. Ohhh brother!"[1] These words capture the ethos and spirit of Black communities who know hardship all too well and the resilience we need to overcome obstacles rooted in systemic oppression. One of the colloquial phrases heard in some Black faith communities is *"Keep on keeping on."* To "keep on keeping on," we need to have hope that we can make it to a better future in spite of any present situation of despair. In the midst of dire circumstances, we need hope to keep going so we can achieve our dreams. In spite of all odds and despite the difficulties of life, we need hope for a better today and a better tomorrow so that we can keep going to accomplish and achieve what we believe to be our ultimate purpose during our finite time on earth.[2] Yet, there are real life obstacles that stand in the way of our wildest dreams and too often cause us to lose hope. Statistically and experientially, this is true for a large number of Black men. To care for the lives of Black men, this book offers a "Hope to Keep Going"[3] framework for care and counseling that considers the importance of nurturing hope in Black men as a trope true to Black experience and the struggle for liberation. The goal is to help Black men survive, become liberated, heal, and, ultimately, flourish in the world. In light of historical realities and contemporary systems of oppression that impede the survival, liberation, healing, and flourishing of Black men, this book argues that it is not just the responsibility of Black communities to care for Black men. Rather, all people in the human village must play a role in the care of Black men.[4] The following account

1

depicts a hard-to-swallow truth in the struggle for Black male survival, liberation, healing, and flourishing.

August 9, 2014. The scene is Ferguson, Missouri. While walking down Canfield Drive on a sunny day, Michael Brown is fatally shot by Ferguson police officer Darren Wilson. Again? Another victim in a long list of unarmed Black men killed by police officers. Yet, nearly four hours later, onlookers discern that there is something eerie about this scene. Eyes are fixed on American pavement painted with the blood of Michael Brown's dead body. You and I see the disheartening scene with impeccable clarity. Perceptive onlookers realize that America, rightfully so, cares passionately for our police officers and veterans. America, rightfully so, believes that our police officers and veterans matter. America also cares to ensure that all people respect the country's flag and national anthem. Yet, nearly four hours later, America did not care enough to ensure that an ambulance crew tend to Michael Brown's dead body. Nearly four hours later, Michael Brown's body remained lying lifeless on American pavement. Somehow America's caring concern[5] halted in the presence of Michael Brown's living and dead body. It was as if America unashamedly declared that the lives of people living in Black and Brown bodies don't matter.

Nonetheless, America keeps going. Wall Street keeps doing business as usual. Politicians politic. Tenure-track academics can teach and write without real concern for the practical needs of the marginalized. There are mental health therapists who provide mental health services to clients without concern, knowledge, or desire to address America's racist past and present and its implications for the mental health of Black and Brown people. Therapists, deemed fit by America to handle the emotional experiences of Black men, have the privilege to study, train, and become licensed mental health professionals without thoughtfully and critically engaging the inescapable evils of racism, sexism, homophobia, and classism, which continue to negatively impact the minds and material realities of Black men. The absence of critical reflection on the workings of racism, sexism, homophobia, and classism too often leads America to fall short in its ability (or inability) to understand and care for the mental health of Black men. Despite the gloomy reality of America's genocidal treatment of Black men, you and I can choose to see and to listen deeply to the experiences and thoughts of Black men. In this book, we have an opportunity to listen deeply to the experiences of Black men (and the ways that they process their life experiences) in order to create a better future for Black men.

As an African American man, I have had my fair share of disappointments and emotional distress because of the presence of racism in my world.[6] My life has been saturated with moments when I have strategized and labored hard to be heard and accepted as a credible and valued voice in spaces that have not always welcomed nor affirmed my presence and voice as an African American man. This has been particularly true of my experiences in the academy (higher education), clinical training (as a psychotherapist), and everyday life. Thankfully, I grew up in Atlanta during the 1980s and 1990s in an environment that affirmed my authentic Black self. As a first love, music served as an outlet to help me process the joys and frustrations of life. When I played music, nothing else mattered. All was well. Everything would be okay. Further aiding my development as a young Black male in Atlanta was my supportive family and faith community, along with the benefits of growing up near Morehouse College. Growing up in Atlanta and being influenced by the ethos of Morehouse College,[7] I knew that my Atlanta community cared and expected great things from me as a Black man in society. However, my subsequent experiences in life revealed that America, as a whole, is not so richly endowed with safe and nurturing spaces where I, as a Black man, could feel fully affirmed to survive and flourish.

While I learned valuable lessons during my undergraduate and graduate school years, I was inundated by emotional blows stemming from racism's presence in society and academic institutions. I wish it were different. During particular classes, including one at the Northwestern University Family Institute, where colleagues and I studied to fulfill requirements for state licensure to become licensed professional counselors, I felt emotionally devastated after having raised perspectives on psychology from a Black perspective. In one of my classes, a tenured White male professor set the tone during the first class session by stating that we would eventually discuss tough subjects, such as race, later in the semester when we were ready. This approach caught me off guard. In previous classes, I was accustomed to discussing race as a starting point and central part of our scholarly and clinical dialogue. Hence, my internal response to the professor's words were: "What's so tough about discussing race? I'm ready now."

As a requirement for the class, we had to participate in a Tavistock Group Relations conference at Northwestern University. The Tavistock conference conducts research and seeks to help conference participants learn about group relations while reflecting on power and authority. Staff at the Tavistock conference facilitates groups and guides participants to an understanding of what is happening in the "Here and Now." Participants are part of a large group (with all conference participants) and smaller breakout groups. I was the only Black male in my breakout group (and one of three Black men—that I can recall—in the entire conference). Participating as the only Black male in my breakout group deeply affected my experience of the "Here and Now." A task of the breakout group was to get to know each other and share our experiences of each other in the "Here and Now." As I began sharing my experiences with the group, members of the group grew irritated because I shared my experience of the "Here and Now" from my perspective as a Black person living in the United States. Members of the group expressed that they wanted to get to know me in the "Here and Now" apart from historical and social context. However, the "Here and Now" of that moment felt oppressive to me because we had to play by the rules of White normativity in the process of getting to know one another, which meant that the group did not want me to express how my experience as a Black person in the world (including the ways that Black people are imagined and treated by others) affected my experience of the "Here and Now." Attempting to break out of the oppressiveness of this moment, I tried sharing parts of my life story, hoping that the group (consisting of current and future therapists) would appreciate my life story and embody empathy and extend compassion towards me, and the lives of other Black people, now that they were more aware of the ways that social context affected my experience of the "Here and Now." However, instead of taking seriously the historical and cultural factors shaping my experience in the "Here and Now," the group continued in its growing frustration because I would not share myself with the group in the ways that they had hoped. They adamantly declared that sharing "all that other stuff" prevented them from getting to know me in the "Here and now." As a person who had engaged in years of my own therapy and sought to embody a reflective and self-aware disposition, I was disturbed by the extent to which the group passionately attempted to separate social context from my identity and experience as a Black person in the "Here and Now." The group wanted to divorce history and cultural context from my identity, personality, and experience in the "Here and Now." Here is the point of my reflective exposition: Although I am the primary author of this book, I, too, have experienced the challenges of living life as a Black man in American society in a way that is similar to some of the experiences of Black men in this book. While the Northwestern University Family Institute has been a helpful re-source for exposing students to a variety of clinical and community settings, as well as offering effective therapeutic services, my visceral memory of emotional devastation remains.

Equally as important, I have needed to remain vigilant of the ways that sexism has granted me privilege. In this sense, while I have experienced moments of disadvantage because of racism's impact on society, I have been unfairly advantaged in certain settings because of sexism's impact on soci-ety. It is, therefore, my responsibility to reflect continually upon the ways that I have been unconsciously shaped by and granted unearned access to opportunities because of patriarchy's impact in the world. I must work ac-tively to resist this form of oppression that is harmful to women, which also negatively compromises the identities of men. Reflection on Black male experience must always embody an intersectional approach that continually reflects on the ways that racism, sexism, homophobia, classism, and religious experience shape the identities and mental processes of Black men.

The primary research questions guiding this book, therefore, ask: How do Black men deal with intrapsychic feelings of invisibility, hyper-visibility, and devaluation, as well as, the hyper-visible images of Black masculinity in contemporary culture? Further, do Black men embody sexist ideology as they deal with the realities of life as a Black man in the United States? As the field research of this project developed, it became clear that an additional appropriate question to consider would be: What do Black men experience in the psyche as they try to make sense of life, survive, and thrive amidst an American culture that views Black men as a problem?[8]

In this book, I argue that spiritual care, counseling, and community leadership most effectively nurture survival, liberation, healing, and human flourishing in Black men and society when a comprehensive approach to care is embodied that takes seriously the experiences of Black men as a starting point. Such an approach must also engage a womanist critique of culture that informs our understandings of Black male identity and draw upon the collective wisdom of critical race theory, Black psychology, Black pastoral theology, and a critical appropriation of psychodynamic theory.

While I am concerned with Black male experience, this book also claims that spiritual caregivers, mental health professionals, and community leaders need to maintain an awareness of the ways that patriarchy negatively affects Black male identity and compromises the ways that Black men relate to Black women and to one another. Maintaining an awareness of the ways that racism, sexism, homophobia, and classism negatively affect Black male experience, this book strives to uncover new possibilities for the survival, liberation, healing, and human flourishing of Black men.

HUMAN FLOURISHING AND ITS BARRIERS

Racism, sexism, homophobia, and classism too often continue to prevent Black men in the United States and throughout the world from surviving and flourishing as their authentic selves. My interest in human flourishing originates from my reading of Victor Anderson's book, *Beyond Ontological Blackness,*[9] where he argues that while suffering and resistance are important for Black people, all human beings, including Black people, want to flourish. Similarly, while holding firmly to the need to resist racism, sexism, homophobia, and classism, I agree with Anderson's view that Black people deserve to live without being relegated to an existence tied solely to suffering and resistance. Black men deserve fair opportunities to survive *and* flourish in the world. While flourishing is the goal of the Hope to Keep Going framework of care and counseling offered in this book, scholars, such as Lee H. Butler, Jr. advocate for the need to first survive in an American genocidal system intent on the dehumanization of Black people. Butler notes that "One can only thrive after one has survived and overcome trauma."[10] In line with Butler's thought, a Hope to Keep Going framework for care and counseling affirms that survival is a prerequisite to flourishing. Consequently, sufficient attention must be given to helping Black men survive before flourishing is possible. Building on Victor Anderson's and Evelyn Parker's notion of human flourishing, this book advocates for a solidarity with Black people to nurture the flourishing of Black men.

My working definition of human flourishing takes its cue from Anderson's critique of ontological Blackness and Parker's reflections on emancipatory hope. It is, therefore, helpful to review Anderson's and Parker's thoughts on human flourishing.

Anderson defines ontological Blackness as "a covering term that connotes categorical, essentialist, and representational languages depicting black life and experience."[11] Critiquing ontological Blackness, he expresses that it "signifies the blackness that whiteness created."[12] For Anderson,

> Ontological blackness is a philosophy of racial consciousness. It is governed by dialectical matrices that existentially structure African Americans' self-conscious perceptions of black life. Under ontological blackness, the conscious lives of blacks are experiences as bound by unresolved binary dialectics of slavery and freedom, negro and citizen, insider and outsider, black and white, struggle and survival. However, such binary polarities admit no possibility of transcendence or mediation.[13]

Hence, "devotion to ontological blackness, its categories and its interests in racial solidarity, loyalty, and authenticity, conceals, subjugates, and calls into question African Americans' interests in fulfilled individuality."[14] Therefore, "Pressing beyond ontological blackness to a new cultural politics of difference requires more than aesthetic criticism."[15] Instead of aesthetic criticism, Anderson advocates for cultural and religious criticism. He observes that

> Cultural criticism does not merely describe the dark sides of social activity, but it resists the temptation toward cynicism by reasserting and affirming creative possibilities for human flourishing . . . Cultural criticism is constructive when it sees among the moral ruins of our contemporary societies possibilities for human flourishing and possibilities for realizing our political, social, and spiritual ideals.[16]

To attain human flourishing, Anderson asserts that one must resist categorical racism and White racial ideology. Categorical racism "appropriates a species logic in which every individual member of a species shares essential traits that identify the member within the species."[17] Historically, Anderson points out, "European philosophers developed a philosophy of difference in terms of rationality, aesthetics, morals, and race."[18] Hence, "European intellectuals sought to disclose European genius as an explanatory category for the progressive, historical movement of the modern age. Categorical racism allowed these intellectuals to legitimize the modern age in terms of comparative cultural anthropology."[19] In addition to naming the problematic nature of categorical racism, Anderson outlines three functions of White racial ideology:

1. It justified the supremacy of European consciousness on a comparative and hence a scientific basis;
2. It provided historical and moral rationalizations for the spread of European imperialism throughout the world; and
3. It justified the exclusion of blacks and other colonized peoples from civic republican citizenship.[20]

Anderson links categorical racism to White racial ideology in naming that "pervasive influences of categorical racism undergird a white racial ideology that justified the exclusion of blacks from the openings of democratic culture. The African presence in America is a racialized *other* whose blackness constitutes a fundamental natural inequality."[21] Therefore, categorical racism and White racial ideology position Black men to be seen and related to as unequal *others*. However, Anderson does not want Black people to have an identity solely tied to the need to resist categorical racism and White racial ideology; such an identity and way of being in the world submits to the norms of ontological Blackness. Anderson crystallizes his critique of ontological Blackness and argument *for* human flourishing in the following statement:

> If suffering and resistance continue to have a totalizing function in womanist theological discourse as they do in classical black theology and Afrocentric theologies, on what does transcendence depend? At what point do thriving and flourishing enter the equation of suffering and resistance? . . . We all want more than to survive . . . We also want to thrive and flourish.[22]

A Hope to Keep Going framework for care and counseling strives to nurture caring communities that cultivate the survival *and* flourishing of Black men.

Evelyn Parker provides a second reference for my working definition of human flourishing. She describes human flourishing as "a state of being in the world that is more than mere existence, but rather, experiencing a quality of life that results from 'a pattern of strivings over a period of time.'" [23] Human flourishing, therefore, is a "process that is nurtured over time, given the optimum conditions. It is our coming forth in the fullness of our God-given potential."[24, 25] In addition to human flourishing being a process that is nurtured over time, it entails commitments to covenantal relationships between the divine, other people, and ourselves. Human flourishing "occurs when the covenantal relationships or promises between God, other people, and ourselves are functioning appropriately . . . faithfulness to the covenantal relationship obligates us to act in ways that institute and maintain human flourishing for all people, especially for the poor, weak, and vulnerable."[26]

Parker sees injustice as a barrier to human flourishing because it "hinders people from coming forth in the fullness of their God-given potential and breaks the divine covenant between God, others, and ourselves. These are situations and decisions that impede the flourishing of an individual or a group of people."[27] In this sense, injustice impedes human flourishing by discouraging people from relating to Black men in life-affirming and authentic ways. This dynamic between Black men and the rest of the world limits Black men from actualizing their full potential. When Black men experience injustice, those in positions of power and those in direct relationship with Black men are not in relationship with them in a way that nurtures hope for them to reach their full potential. This is not to diminish the importance of Black men taking responsibility to actualize their full potential; rather, it is crucial that those in power and those in direct relationship with Black men work to dismantle injustice so that Black men have additional life-affirming opportunities to survive and flourish.

Building on Anderson's and Parker's reflections, I identify the following ten tenets of human flourishing which must be nurtured in and among Black men, according to a Hope to Keep Going framework for care and counseling: 1) Knowing and loving oneself deeply—including one's own personality, family, and racial-ethnic heritage; 2) Feeling supported by life-affirming community; 3) Committing to life-affirming covenantal relationships with the divine, other people, and self. This includes cultivating life-affirming faith and spirituality that fosters deep connection with self, one's ancestors, the divine, the global human community, and living creatures throughout the world. Such a faith and spirituality establishes, develops, and maintains local, national, and global cultures of justice and peace; 4) Relating to others with respect, empathy, and caring concern; 5) Acknowledging and valuing difference among human beings; 6) Having fair opportunities to thrive in educational environments[28] that equip one with skills necessary to achieve career success and contribute to the liberation of unjust societies, while having access to material resources needed to live a comfortable life above the poverty line. This includes fair opportunities to attain meaningful work and economic stability; 7) Consciously participating in society-at-large at the local, city, state, national, and/or global level; 8) Embodying and maintaining a vision of oneself free from the grips of categorical racism, white racial ideology, sexist ideology, homophobic ideology, classist ideology, and all other forms of xenophobic ideology; 9) Taking proper care of one's physical body; and 10) Discovering and connecting with a life purpose greater than oneself.

As a result of the legacy and modern-day presence of racism, sexism, homophobia, and classism in society, attaining human flourishing has been elusive for many Black men and women living in the United States. Consequently, Black men need a comprehensive approach to care and counseling to nurture their flourishing. Due to the obstacles to survival and flourishing, Black men need astute caregivers and counselors who operate out of a comprehensive, Hope to Keep Going, approach to care and counseling, which explicitly acknowledges and aims to dismantle racism, sexism, homophobia, and classism in their lives. A comprehensive approach to care and counseling takes seriously history, culture, and intrapsychic experience. Such an approach, for instance, acknowledges the unjust deaths of Black men and women killed in the streets of the United States as factors affecting the mental health of Black men. From Emmett Till to Tamir Rice, Rekia Boyd, Michael Brown, Tanisha Anderson, and Sandra Bland, unarmed Black men and women continue to be gunned down and killed by police. How do these images impact the psyches of Black men? How do Black men handle these images roaming in their unconscious and conscious thoughts? Feelings of hurt, wounded-ness, anger, and rage are surely primed and ready to spread like fire shut up in one's bones. As a result, Black men have lived as people without power in the American imagination, except for unhealthy embodiments of power such as sexual prowess and domination over women. A comprehensive, Hope to Keep Going, approach to care and counseling acknowledges that Black men have also operated out of identities that embody unhealthy constructions of power, which perpetuate cultures of male dominance and privilege detrimental to the mental health and overall well-being of Black women. Kumea Shorter-Gooden explained it this way: "In fact, Black men are disproportionately both perpetrators of violence and victims of violence."[29] Acknowledging that Black men are both victims and perpetrators of violence is necessary for the work of freeing Black men from unhealthy models of Black masculinity. For instance, a Hope to Keep Going model of care and counseling takes seriously nurturing in Black men a passion and desire to care for Black women as an essential dimension of Black masculinity. Too many Black women are devalued by Black men, as evident by the prevalence of intimate partner violence against women. While intimate partner violence is not the sole focus of this book, a Hope to Keep Going framework for care and counseling takes seriously intimate partner violence. It is essential for constructions and understandings of Black masculinity to hear the voices of Black women and reduce the inevitable likelihood that the forces of sexism will prevail in our concepts of Black masculinity. Sexist and machoistic visions of Black masculinity are life-denying and must be intentionally and actively resisted in a Hope to Keep Going framework of care and counseling.

BY THE NUMBERS: STATISTICAL DATA

Statistics verify our awareness that Black men are both victims and perpetrators of violence. Racism causes Black men to live as oppressed people in the realms of formal education, mass incarceration, police brutality, health disparities, and unemployment. Injustice in these key areas too often prevents Black men from flourishing. The following statistics highlight the ways that Black men do not flourish in contemporary American society.[30]

Black Male Educational Achievement

According to a report by the Schott Foundation, the graduation rate in the state of Illinois was 58.6 percent for Black males compared to 85.2 percent for White males.[31] In the city of Chicago, the graduation rate for Black males was 41 percent and 64 percent for White males, showing a 23 percent gap between the high school graduation rates of Black males and White males. The disparity of suspension and expulsion rates between Blacks and Whites also reveals a stark contrast as the study reported that nationally 15 percent of Black males were suspended compared to 5 percent of White males. The national average rate of expulsion for Black males was 0.61 percent compared to 0.21 percent for White males. The Schott Foundation named school suspensions as a leading factor that introduces students to the school-to-prison pipeline.

Police Brutality

Police brutality against Black men and women, as acknowledged by the Black Lives Matter movement, has also prevented Black men from flourishing. A study in *The Guardian* reported that 1,134 people died at the hands of police officers in 2015 and observed that "Young black men were nine times more likely than other Americans to be killed by police officers in 2015."[32] *The Guardian* reported that approximately 25 percent of Blacks killed were unarmed, compared to 17 percent of Whites.

Unemployment

Disproportionate unemployment rates are another aspect of injustice preventing Black men from flourishing. According to the U.S. Department of Labor's *Bureau of Labor Statistics*, 10.1 percent of Black males ages 25–34 were unemployed in the first quarter of 2016 while 4.9 percent of White males of the same age group were unemployed.[33] In the 35–44 age group, 8.4 percent of Black males were unemployed compared to 3.6 percent of White males.

Intimate Partner Violence

The three categories named above—education, police brutality, and unemployment—illustrate concrete ways that Black men are systemically oppressed in the United States. Equally important are reflections on the ways that Black men exert power to oppress women. Men are the primary perpetrators of intimate partner violence against women. A caregiver and counselor operating out of a Hope to Keep Going framework for care and counseling, therefore, intentionally listens for ways that a Black man embodies masculinity to prevent adoption of Black masculinities that perpetuate intimate partner violence against women and other men. In the case where a Black man embraces toxic masculinity that enacts violence upon women and other men, the caregiver or counselor should challenge such a masculinity and work with the Black male care receiver to dismantle the toxic masculinity operative in his life and in the life of the culture in which he lives. Intimate partner violence is enacted in, at minimum, three forms: 1) physical abuse; 2) sexual abuse; and 3) emotional abuse. According to a survey conducted by the U.S. Department of Justice, "violence against women is predominantly male violence: All women who were raped since age 18 were raped by a male."[34] The U.S. Department of Justice reports that the number of women raped by a female since the age of 18 was not large enough to calculate reliable estimates. Even more striking, "The vast majority (91.9 percent) of women who were physically assaulted since age 18 were assaulted by a male, while only 11.8 percent were physically assaulted by a female."[35] Additionally, the report reveals the disproportionate number of women who experience intimate partner violence compared to the number of men who experience intimate partner violence. "Women experience more intimate partner violence than do men: 22.1 percent of surveyed women, compared with 7.4 percent of surveyed men, reported they were physically assaulted by a current or former spouse, cohabiting partner, boyfriend or girlfriend, or date in their lifetime."[36] This begs the question: Why do women experience intimate partner violence at nearly three times the rate of men? I argue that one factor is that Black men need to exhibit greater empathy, compassion, support, and overall care for the lives of women. In the Black community, according to the U.S. Department of Justice's report, 18.8 percent of African American women in the study responded that they have been raped compared to 3.3 percent of African American men. Embracing the spirit of Ubuntu,[37] Black men and the larger community need to care deeply for Black women, and all women, so the conditions under which rape occurs will be removed. Additionally, Black men need to embody a masculine identity that cares deeply for the needs, including emotional experiences, of survivors of rape. A Hope to Keep Going framework for care and counseling is not complete without advocating for the survival and flourishing of Black women, and all women.

FOCUS OF BOOK

This book focuses on the experiences of Black men ages 25–40 who lived in the city of Chicago, Illinois, at the time of this study. Their experiences are positioned at the starting point of our discussion on the mental well-being of Black men because the lived experiences of Black people have too often been excluded in our theories of care and counseling. The interviews in this study were conducted with Black men in order to continue the conversation on the care of Black men already engaged in by scholars, clinicians, and everyday people so that a subsequent grounded theory might emerge for spiritual care, counseling, and community leadership that is rooted in contemporary Black men's experiences and in dialogue with critical race theory, womanist thought, Black psychology, a critical appropriation of psychodynamic theory, and Black pastoral theology. The interviews were conducted to engage research participants in authentic and thoughtful reflection about their lives as Black men living in the United States. I am touched by their lives and the ways that they trusted me enough to open up and share intimate and, at times, vulnerable aspects of their life stories. I value their trust and have attempted to tell their stories with care and respect so that we can have a fruitful dialogue to improve the care of Black men. As we connect with their stories, we have the opportunity to listen deeply to the music of their lives.[38] This music is soulful, painful, resilient, and, at times, hopeful. The music of their lives contains complex riffs that will stir our souls if we listen deeply with hearts of compassion. As the music of their lives unfolds in these pages (and as we listen deeply to the music of our own lives), we embark on a caring journey into their worlds and dialogue with key thinkers who help us grapple with themes that emerged from the experiences of Black men in this book.

APPROACH

To increase our understanding of Black men, I have adopted an eclectic method that draws from the collective wisdom of Black male research participants, theoreticians, and creativity[39] to develop a theory of care that is free of the constraints of White normativity. The qualitative research presented in this book adopts aspects of Kathy Charmaz's constructivist grounded theory and reveals eight themes that emerged from my conversations with Black men in this book. While eight themes emerged, concentrated attention (in the form of a chapter per theme) is given to three of the eight themes in chapters one, three, and four. The other five themes remain on the periphery of our discussion. I have selected the three themes for primary focus to give us insight into the phenomena occurring in the lives of Black men to increase our knowledge of spiritual care, counseling, and community leadership with Black men. The theories presented in chapter two were selected because they resonate with the themes that emerged from the interviews with research participants. The hope is that this comprehensive approach will help us more effectively care for the mental health of Black men.

OUTLINE OF CHAPTERS

Chapters one, three, four, and five present the narratives of Black men, with chapter five pointing to a Hope to Keep Going framework for care and counseling. In chapter two, I survey theories that resonate with the empirical data in this study. The chapter includes Derrick Bell's, Angela Harris', and Emma Jordan's critical race perspectives; Stephen Ray's framing of race as religious discourse; Michelle Wallace's and Chanequa Walker-Barnes' womanist critique; R. L'Heureux Lewis-McCoy's critique of Black male privilege; the work of W. E. B. Du Bois; and Katrina Bell's analysis of masculinity and the media. Chapters six and seven continue reflection on a Hope to Keep Going framework for care and counseling by offering communal and individual models of change, respectively, to pave a path forward to care optimally for the mental well-being of Black men.

METHODOLOGY

There are moments in history that cry out for new discoveries of qualitative research that can inform the development of newly grounded theories. Our current age—one that is impacted by Black Lives Matter and other movements—is such a moment that calls for continual reflection upon the ways that we imagine care for Black men. This is a moment when we must embrace the spirit of creativity[40] and listen deeply to the lived experiences and intrapsychic experiences of Black men and women. In this sense, I privilege qualitative inquiry over purely descriptive accounts of Black life to help us empathically connect with the life experiences and intrapsychic experiences of Black men.

Qualitative inquiry helps us pause from the busyness of life and listen deeply to experiences and voices that we might otherwise overlook. To hear the voices of marginalized and disregarded Black men, I followed tenets of Kathy Charmaz's constructivist grounded theory. Charmaz's constructivist grounded theory provides a helpful way to engage the care of Black men because it enables us to acknowledge the subjectivity of both researcher and research participants in the construction of grounded theory. In other words, the researcher and author are not objective and all-knowing observers. As Charmaz notes, "If . . . we start with the assumption that social reality is multiple, processual, and constructed, then we must take the researcher's position, privileges, perspective, and interactions into account as an inherent part of the research reality. It, too, is a construction."[41]

In the spirit of acknowledging my own subjectivity, I offer the following as a window into my soul. I am a Black man in my thirties from Atlanta, Georgia, raised in a Church of God faith community with national headquarters in Anderson, Indiana. I have reflected critically on my embedded theology, which developed as a result of my childhood experiences in the Church of God movement and faith community. I have since embraced an intentional theology informed by my experiences in the world and by my exposure to diverse theological, psychological, critical race, womanist, and other intellectual discourses while seeking to maintain life-giving aspects of the Church of God tradition and faith community which shaped me. I am the oldest of four siblings and have two fathers. One of my fathers is my biological father, Jimmy Orange, and the other my step-dad, Arthur Grier, whom I refer to as "dad" because of his presence in my life as a father-figure that contributed to my development as a man. He entered my life as a father-figure and married my mom, Grace Elizabeth Dennis Grier, when I was five years old. All these experiences, and many others, including my study of racism, sexism, homophobia, psychology, theology, and community leadership, inform my perspective and approach to the care of Black men.

RECRUITING CONVERSATION PARTNERS

Having acknowledged my own subjectivity, I want to offer a brief word about how I recruited the men in this book. To recruit Black male participants for this book, I visited two barbershops in Chicago's Hyde Park neighborhood and invited Black men between the ages of 25–40 to participate. I aimed to recruit a small sample size to explore the experiences of their lives with depth. Hence, the stories of five passionate Black men are told throughout this book. It bears mentioning that the owners of the barbershops were tremendously helpful in recruiting Black men for this project. Once the owners agreed to participate in this project and publicly announced their support of it, men in the two barbershops eagerly signed up and agreed to participate. I raise the important role of the barbershop owners to emphasize that their support and public affirmation mattered and was a critical factor in successfully recruiting Black men to participate in this project.

The following parameters were set as requirements for Black men to participate in the interviews of this study: Research participants must not have an annual income that exceeds $75,000 per year. Additionally, they must have completed a G.E.D., high school diploma, or bachelor's degree. Men with graduate degrees were not eligible to participate in this study. The men must have also lived in the city of Chicago at the time of the study and have at least one parent who is African American. I selected the income and educational parameters named above to highlight the experiences of middle and lower socioeconomic status Black men who experience life without the resources of graduate education. These parameters were set with the perspective that greater financial and educational resources can position one to be shielded from *some* of the blows of a racist, sexist, homophobic, and classist social environment. However, because the category of race and the working of racism continue to exist in social constructions of reality, no Black person is immune to unjust treatment.

A WORD ON THE FOCUS GROUP

I chose to use only data from the individual interviews to conduct line-by-line coding and construct themes identified for this book. However, data from the focus group is used as peripheral knowledge to provide a fuller picture of the lives of Black men. Because of the energy exuded in the focus group, which was slightly different than that of the individual interviews, it is helpful to name key moments from the focus group.

During the focus group, the men were very engaged in conversation with each other and exuded a tremendous amount of passion as they reflected on their own life experiences and challenges as Black men living in contemporary society. Their passionate energy displayed during the focus group was more intense than the energy they displayed during their individual interviews. Compared to their individual interviews, they opened up more readily in the focus group concerning police brutality, street life, and gang activity. There was tremendous synergy and flow amongst the men on these issues. For example, research participant Eddie[42] opened up more readily about personal matters in the focus group than he did during his individual interviews and expressed that he was hurt because his father was absent in his life. Kendrick's and Eddie's personalities were more outgoing and less reserved during the focus group compared to their individual interviews. They appeared more relaxed during the focus group. Kendrick's dry, direct, and blunt sense of humor was on full display during the focus group. He used his sense of humor passionately to drive home points about the injustices facing Black men. While Kendrick and Eddie displayed a slightly more outgoing and relaxed personality during the focus group than during their individual interviews, I did not see much of a difference in the personalities of Matthew and Kevin[43] during the focus group compared to their individual interviews. It bears mentioning that Darrell and Jamal were not present during the focus group, yet their individual interviews were included during the coding of themes from the individual interviews of all five research participants who met the parameters set for this project.

The men also named musical artists, politicians, and social leaders during the focus group as having a significant impact on their lives. Kanye West, Mike Myers, George Bush, Tupac, and Huey Newton were a few of the figures in pop culture, political leadership, and social leadership mentioned during the focus group. Such references are evidence that politicians, leaders of social movements, and popular artists significantly impact the psyches of Black men.

Overall, during the focus group, the men exhibited collective frustration about the ways that Black men are treated by police, the government, and society-at-large. This frustration grew as conversation in the focus group continued to unfold. A growing rage filled the room as they passionately discussed police brutality against Black men. For example, Kendrick referred to the shooting of Trayvon Martin and asked, "Why Zimmerman[44] isn't in for life? Why doesn't he have life in jail? That's what I'm tripp'n on." In response to the Zimmerman verdict and the injustices facing Black people in the United States, Eddie asked, "What do you expect us to do?"

Amidst the growing rage, there were moments when laughter filled the room as the men and I shared moments of comic relief. We bonded and engaged in conversation as a closely knit group. As the intensity of the conversation progressed, debate emerged among the men over the best approach Black people should take to resist systemic oppression. Kendrick said, "No, you can't take the MLK approach. You gotta take the Malcolm X approach." The group eventually agreed that it is important to have a mass movement of multiple leaders to resist and overcome systemic oppression. They discussed the government's actions of infiltrating gangs as an example of what happens when the head of a movement is taken out, expressing that "chaos" emerges when there is an absence of structure in organizations such as gangs.

Reflection on the focus group also revealed that men in this book are passionate about caring for Black male youth. While a couple of the men discussed the importance of caring for their daughters, future studies will benefit from continuing to explore the dynamics of Black men raising their daughters.[45] The men in this book also expressed an appreciation for participating in this project because they believed it was something positive. Kendrick stated, "I chose [to participate] because I'm glad you're doing something positive. I'd rather help my brother out." He appreciated "helping [me] out and just discussing, and getting things out," and affirmed that "this is constructive. I like doing this." Matthew, Kendrick, Kevin, and Eddie each acknowledged that I was in the process of getting my PhD at the time of the study and were very affirming of my pursuits. At the conclusion of the focus group, I thanked the owner of the barbershop for opening his shop for the focus group on a night when the barbershop ordinarily would have been closed. The other men quickly expressed their gratitude to the owner for opening his space and being present with us during the focus group. In response, the owner expressed tremendous support for the men and the research project by saying, "It sounds like you guys did a wonderful job. Yeah, I just wanted to sit back and let you do your work . . . it sounds like you all gon' do a real good job. So I thank you all for coming."

CONTRIBUTION

This book deeply engages the cultural and intrapsychic experiences of Black men and dialogues with key thinkers to understand and dismantle racism, sexism, homophobia, classism, their impacts, and to make possible survival, liberation, healing, and human flourishing for Black men in the United States of America. The aim of this book is to pave a way forward to continue imagining and re-imagining liberated Black male identities that are not limited and strained by racism, sexism, heteronormativity, homophobia, classism, and religious bigotry. This book is written as a resource to nurture hope to keep going in the lives of Black men so that we will survive and flourish emotionally, spiritually, materially, and in our relationships with others.

NOTES

1. Robert Adetuyi and Gregory Anderson. *Stomp the Yard*. DVD. Directed by Sylvain White. Culver City: Sony Pictures, 2007.

2. I acknowledge that there are multiple perspectives that affirm that our current lifetime is not the only one life that we have or will experience, such as reincarnation and other perspectives on the afterlife. Yet, for the purposes of maximizing our potentials in the current lifetime, I am suggesting that all persons need hope in a better tomorrow to keep going in order to survive, experience liberation from oppressive realities, experience healing from the things that have wounded us, and flourish. I am particularly concerned with cultivating the survival, liberation, healing, and flourishing of the most vulnerable and marginalized people in the world.

3. I will use Hope to Keep Going without quotation marks in the remaining pages as the title for the framework of care and counseling presented in this book.

4. It is the responsibility of the human village to care for all people, particular the most marginalized and vulnerable people in our midst. Yet, for the sake of the purpose of this book, I focus attention on the responsibility of the human village to care for the lives of Black men.

5. In this use of the term "America," I am referring to White America which continues to be guided by the ideology of White supremacy, White superiority, and White normativity. Certainly there are Black and Brown people (and White people who actively work to resist White supremacy, White superiority, and White normativity) who care for Michael Brown's body and the many other unarmed Black and Brown women and men who have been unjustly

killed, tortured, humiliated, blocked from access to resources needed to survive and flourish, and otherwise terrorized in the United States of America and across the globe.

6. Having experienced disappointment and emotional distress due to the manifestations of racism, I should note that these experiences don't dictate my entire existence. I am thankful to have had a supportive family and community growing up in Atlanta, Georgia. This supportive environment has been an emotional foundation and resource which has helped me experience moments of joy throughout my life. Because of the memory and access to this supportive environment, I have an internal resource that has helped me live into the future with a healthy sense of self-worth as a Black person in spite of otherwise toxic racist environments in various contexts in the United States.

7. Growing up in close proximity to Morehouse College, for me, meant that I could be Black and proud. Black excellence was the standard. Because of the legacy of not only Morehouse College but, also, Spelman College, Clark Atlanta University, and Morris Brown College, I grew up in an environment in which I was surrounded by educated Black people who also cared dearly to give back to their community. This was my world. In such a world, I felt loved, respected, and sensed that the world expected me to give 110 percent of myself to achieve Black excellence and make a positive difference in the world.

8. Here I am referring to W. E. B. Du Bois' question, "How does it feel to be a problem?" in *The Souls of Black Folk* (1903 original ed.; New York: Barnes & Nobles Classics, 2005), 7.

9. Victor Anderson, *Beyond Ontological Blackness: An Essay on African American Religious and Cultural Criticism* (New York: The Continuum Publishing Company, 1995).

10. Lee Butler, Jr., *Liberating Our Dignity, Saving Our Souls: A New Theory of African American Identity Formation* (St. Louis: Chalice Press, 2006), 106.

11. Victor Anderson, *Beyond Ontological Blackness: An Essay on African American Religious and Cultural Criticism* (New York: The Continuum Publishing Company, 1995), 11.

12. Anderson, *Beyond Ontological Blackness*, 13.

13. Anderson, *Beyond Ontological Blackness,* 14.

14. Anderson, *Beyond Ontological Blackness*, 15.

15. Anderson, *Beyond Ontological Blackness*, 17.

16. Anderson, *Beyond Ontological Blackness*, 28.

17. Anderson, *Beyond Ontological Blackness*, 51.

18. Anderson, *Beyond Ontological Blackness,* 52.

19. Anderson, *Beyond Ontological Blackness,* 52.

20. Anderson, *Beyond Ontological Blackness,* 52.

21. Anderson, *Beyond Ontological Blackness*, 78.

22. Anderson, *Beyond Ontological Blackness*, 112.

23. Evelyn Parker, *Trouble Don't Last Always: Emancipatory Hope Among African American Adolescents* (Cleveland: The Pilgrim Press, 2003), 152.

24. Parker, *Trouble Don't Last Always*, 152.

25. Parker's definition of human flourishing includes a spirituality that maintains commitment to social justice. Her notion of spirituality weaves together religious beliefs "with practices of social justice (Parker, p. 22)." Hence, "This type of spirituality manifests itself in a seamless life of divine and human activity against economic, political, and racial dominance (Parker, p. 22)."

26. Parker, *Trouble Don't Last Always,* 151–152.

27. Parker, *Trouble Don't Last Always,* 152.

28. Educational environments include trade school, college or university, and other forms of apprenticeship which enables one to achieve this tenet of human flourishing.

29. Kumea Shorter-Gooden, "Therapy with African American Men and Women," *Handbook of African American Psychology,* ed. Helen Neville, Brendesha Tynes, and Shawn Utsey (Thousand Oaks: Sage Publications, Inc., 2009), 447.

30. In the instances where state statistics are provided, I reference statistics from Illinois because the research participants in this book lived in the city of Chicago, Illinois, at the time of this study.

31. Schott Foundation for Public Education, "State Graduation Data," accessed May 11, 2016, http://blackboysreport.org/national-summary/state-graduation-data/#.

32. Jon Swaine, Oliver Laughland, Jamiles Lartey, Ciara McCarthy, "Young black men killed by U.S. police at highest rate in year of 1,134 deaths," The Guardian, accessed May 11, 2016, http://www.theguardian.com/us-news/2015/dec/31/the-counted-police-killings-2015-young-black-men.

33. U.S. Department of Labor, *Labor Force Statistics from the Current Population Survey*, Bureau of Labor Statistics, accessed May 11, 2016, http://www.bls.gov/web/empsit/cpsee_e16.htm.

34. U.S. Department of Justice, *Full Report of the Prevalence, Incidence, and Consequences of Violence Against Women: Findings From the National Violence Against Women Survey*, by Patrician Tjaden and Nancy Thoennes, Office of Justice Programs (Washington D.C., 2000).

35. U.S. Department of Justice, *Full Report of the Prevalence, Incidence, and Consequences of Violence Against Women.*

36. U.S. Department of Justice, *Full Report of the Prevalence, Incidence, and Consequences of Violence Against Women.*

37. *Ubuntu* is an African term often translated as "I am what I am because of who we are."

38. *Music of their lives / Music of our lives*—a metaphor I develop and use which acknowledges: 1) the intricacies and totality of a person's lived experiences 2) the ways that he or she makes meaning of those experiences and 3) the ways that he or she desires to live into the future. I often encourage my students of spiritual care and counseling to listen deeply to the music of a person's and a community's life in order to offer optimal care and counseling with individuals and communities.

39. Emmanuel Lartey notes that creativity is an aspect of postcolonial activity in his book *Postcolonializing God.* I have adopted the spirit of postcoloniality, as outlined by Lartey, as part of the ethos of my approach to care and counseling.

40. Here I am using *creativity* in the postcolonial sense of the word as defined by Emmanuel Lartey in his book, *Postcolonializing God.*

41. Charmaz, *Constructing Grounded Theory,* 13.

42. All five Black male research participants, including Eddie, are formally introduced at the beginning of chapter one.

43. While Kevin was a delightful person and participated in the focus group, conversation from his individual interviews were not factored into the coding of themes for this book because his demographic information was outside of the parameters set for research participants in this study. However, his narrative is presented in a vignette in Appendix A.

44. George Zimmerman fatally shot Trayvon Martin in February 2012 and was acquitted of all charges in July 2013.

45. Scholars such as Lee H. Butler have explored this topic. An example of literature on Black men caring for their daughters can be found in Butler's multi-authored book, *Listen My Son: Wisdom for African American Fathers.*

Part I

Understanding Context

Chapter One

Chronically Dissed

bell hooks offers a perspective on the realities facing Black men:

> *Sadly, the real truth, which is a taboo to speak, is that this is a culture that does not love black males, that they are not loved by white men, white women, black women, or girls and boys. And that especially most black men do not love themselves. How could they, how could they be expected to love surrounded by so much envy, desire, hate? Black males in the culture of imperialist white-supremacist capitalist patriarchy are feared but they are not loved. . . . If black males were loved they could hope for more than a life locked down, caged, confined; they could imagine themselves beyond containment.* [1]

This chapter engages the stories of Black men whom I had the privilege of interviewing in Chicago in the city's Hyde Park neighborhood. It engages the first theme selected for primary focus in this book: Chronically Disregarded, Disrespected, Discredited, Feared, and Devalued. Let me take a moment to introduce the five Black men in this book. The five Black men who shared their life experiences and perspectives are Matthew, Kendrick, Darrell, Eddie, and Jamal. [2] Matthew is a thirty-six-year-old entrepreneur with a high school diploma. Kendrick is a thirty-five-year-old worker in telecommunications with a bachelor's degree. Darrell is twenty-nine years old with a bachelor's degree and previously worked at a large retail corporation. He is now pursuing entrepreneurship. Eddie is twenty-six years old with a bachelor's degree and intends to begin his graduate education the next academic year. Finally, Jamal is a twenty-five-year-old barber with a high school diploma. The annual income of the men ranges from $0–$75,000. All of the men identified themselves as Black men living in the city of Chicago at the time of the study.

As an introduction to this chapter's discussion on the ways that Black men are chronically disregarded, disrespected, discredited, feared, and devalued, it is critical to acknowledge the impact that negative cultural images have had on Black men.[3] Understanding the impact of racism on the lives of Black men is important because, as the fourth edition of *African American Psychology: From Africa to America* points out, "the greater the perceived racism, the greater the likelihood of mental distress, including depression and anxiety."[4] Our conversations revealed that negative cultural images of Black men in the media and society function as barriers that frequently prevent Black men from flourishing. All the men in this study acknowledge the presence of negative cultural images of Black men in the media and society, and said that these images have had significant impact on their thoughts and the thought processes of other Black men. Additionally, they passionately expressed and demonstrated that the media has significant impact on not only the thoughts of Black men, but also the ways that other people view Black men. The following paragraphs highlight the Black men in this study's understanding of: 1) society's perception of Black men; 2) society's expectation of Black men; and 3) society's view of the ultimate life destination of Black men.

First, the men in this study say that society believes Black men are *not educated, dumb, criminals, violent, a threat, evil, thugs,* and *savages.* Matthew expressed that "It's been an intentional criminalization of our culture." Additionally, Darrell shared, "I feel like they focus on African Americans as the worst of the worst. I mean there's a lot of black men. But it's just like, why us? Why pick us? Why pick on us? What did we do? So it's just like those images . . . they portray violent men. Violent. Dumb. We don't know anything." As a whole, the men in this study pointed out that society depicts Black men as being void of emotion and that the lives of Black men have no value. In the words of Eddie, "Our lives don't matter."

Second, the Black men in this book acknowledged the *expectations society has of Black men.* They expressed that society believes Black men can only attain professional success as an entertainer[5] and that other successful life options are not available to Black men. Darrell noted,

> Um, we're always in entertainment. That's all we know is entertainment. Sports. Movies. Just entertainment. You don't see too many black men on TV talking about . . . praising too many black men about lawyers or real-estate investors, Wall Street. You don't see none of that. The only thing you see is entertainment. We either in movies, music, or sports. Those the big three. So as black men growing up, that's all we know. . . . So we don't know any other way. So when we try to go those other ways . . . try to get insight from other people—Caucasians or whoever you trying to go to—It's difficult. They looking at you crazy like, "Why you trying to do that? That's not you." Or it's surprising if you're doing that.

When I asked Jamal to describe the images of Black men he sees in the media, he stated,

> Then again, as I said before, the only good thing about us is unless we're actors, rappers, or you know something of that nature, they never really get to show us . . . like back in the 90s what else, what other things we could be doing? Like you know doctors and things of that nature. You know we have the mindset. We have the capacity to do those things too. So, um, but mostly we're being portrayed as evil people.

Third, an awareness of society's belief of the *ultimate life destination of Black men* is important for an accurate understanding of how culture has an impact on the mental health of Black men. The men in this book expressed that society believes the ultimate life destinations of Black men are limited to being incarcerated, killed by the police, or, as previously mentioned, becoming successful as a professional entertainer. Therefore, Black men who transcend these expectations of Black manhood defy the odds, like the way salmon swim upstream against tumultuous currents. When I asked Kendrick to explain what it means to be a Black man, he said,

> It's a whole lot. You gotta overcome a lot and then sometimes you don't. You gotta play a role sometimes in certain I guess locations, whether you at work or at home. You just gotta learn how to control yourself and don't give people that stereotype. That's what I try to avoid. When they see you they like, "oh he's black." But I have a bachelor's degree and I'm not your typical black guy that you think that you see on TV.

"LOOKED AT LIKE WE'RE MONSTERS" —
CHRONICALLY DISREGARDED, DISRESPECTED,
DISCREDITED, FEARED, AND DEVALUED

Living in an American context that is inundated with negative cultural images, views, and expectations of Black men, the men in this book revealed that they and other Black men are chronically disregarded, disrespected, discredited, feared, and devalued. Rather than define each term, I make space for the voices of Black men to speak for themselves. While exploring how Black men have been treated daily by society, I observed that they have been disregarded, disrespected, discredited, feared, and devalued while walking down the street, at work, in school, with their families, in personal relationships and friendships. Four subthemes can help us unpack the ways that they have been disregarded, disrespected, discredited, feared, and devalued at various points throughout their lives. The four subthemes frequently occurring in their lives are: 1) Not Known; 2) *"Looked at like we're monsters"*; 3)

Questioned and Excluded from the Group; and 4) Expected "to act a certain way."

FREQUENTLY OCCURRING IN
THE LIVES OF BLACK MEN

Not Known

The men in this book expressed that they and other Black men are not known by society. They feel as if the people in their lives do not have an adequate understanding of their identity, personhood, and experiences. As a result, they are related to by others based on society's assumptions of Black men. In this regard, Black men are treated by others based on how Black men are imagined in the minds of others. As a result, Black men are related to, primarily, through the lens of society's imagination of Black men, and not based on adequate understandings and depictions of Black men's experiences and personalities. One can fathom that some in society intentionally choose this method of relating to Black men so as not to be in any authentic and caring relationship with Black men. By choosing not be in authentic and caring relationships with Black men, society eliminates the possibility of knowing Black men. Hence, society alienates Black men as nonhuman figments of its imagination.

Acknowledging how Black men exist in the minds of others he has encountered, Kendrick expressed that there are stereotypes of Black men and believed that it is important for him not to give in to these stereotypes. I asked Kendrick to explain what he meant by stereotypes of Black men. He explained,

> What they portray in the media. Everything you see in the media is what people think. Cuz I remember when I was in the Navy, and we went to Australia, some kids had never seen black people. They saw us and they like, "Puff Daddy." [I said], 'I'm not Puff Daddy.' You know I had some jewelry on, so it's weird when they see you in other countries they assume you're this way until they get to know you. A lot of people react before they start thinking.

Kendrick later elaborated on the assumptions that others have of Black men and described how these assumptions connect to devaluation:

> when people treat you differently that's because they don't know no better. They're going to devalue you. They do it all the time. Like people probably devalue him (referring to a black man sitting in a wheel chair on the sidewalk outside of the restaurant where we sat for our interview. The man is asking for money as people walk along the sidewalk). They don't know him at all but they just gonna treat him a certain way. And you don't know his situation. You

don't know what put him in that situation. But people are going to devalue him just because they look. . . . And that's just basically devaluation based on appearance without knowing nobody. People do that all the time.

"Looked at Like We're Monsters"

Because society does not take the time to get to know Black men, it views Black men through the lens of its imagination. It is clear from conversations with the men in this book that one of the ways that Black men exist in the imaginations of people in society is as monsters. Jamal expressed this perspective directly. During our first interview, Jamal expressed that Black people are treated "a lot less than" other people. Following his lead, I suggested that Black men are "treated a lot less than . . . other folks." Jamal responded,

> Definitely. Uh, how strongly we are looked at [by] the police, [by] other people, like we're monsters or something of that nature, and we're just basically . . . we bleed the same way they do, just try to protect and provide for our families just like they do, just try to get ahead in life like they do. But it seems to be that we're always being the ones looked at in the wrong way in the limelight, unless we're playing basketball or rapping.

Describing a moment when he felt devalued, he noted,

> Um, a time I had felt devalued . . . Um, like I said, I work in Hyde Park, so walking down the street. When I see a person walking towards me and they cross the street or a person that clinches just a little tighter to their purse when I walk closer. . . . Like I said, we are looked down upon by every other race. Uh. Not even respected. But, you know, we seem to persevere and do our thing and uh, stick to our self.

In addition to these reflections from Jamal, Darrell mentioned that Black people stand out in society. I asked him what it's like to stand out as a Black person. Darrell explained that he felt "like it's the worst thing because people look at us like we're so scary as a black man." Both Jamal and Darrell are keenly aware of how they are "looked at" by others in society. For Jamal, Black men are "looked at . . . like we're monsters," while Darrell perceives Black men as being looked at "like we're so scary." Such an experience in the world inevitably has an impact on the psyches of Black men. To cultivate the survival and flourishing of Black men, we must consider and acknowledge the ways that Black men have been chronically "looked at" punitively by people they encounter in the world on a daily basis. Chronic punitive looks toward Black men have the ability and potential to strike damaging blows to the psyches of Black men.

Maintaining an awareness that one is constantly being "looked at" negatively by others affects one's psychological and spiritual experience. Black men are aware of the ways that they are negatively "looked at" by others and may feel in the core of their beings that others are constantly viewing and relating to them through a negative lens in every human interaction. Jamal helps us understand this reality. During our conversation on Black male invisibility, he expressed,

> Uh, I really haven't felt, I guess, to be invisible, other than that fact of, like I said, through society, through other than being looked at like a monster, I guess, to other people when I walk down the street, you know, when I'm just a regular dark person. I wouldn't say I feel invisible. I would say I feel like I'm being pointed at every second of my life. I'm everything but invisible actually. Uh, and like I said, all I try to do is what's right, you know. Because I'm under that microscope. Like I said, when you are doing something in your life, even being black, there is no such thing as invisible. You're always being looked at by someone somewhere.

Jamal and the other Black men in this book help us see how Black men are hyper-visible in American society. Because literature in Black psychology and other writings noted invisibility as a core psychological issue facing Black men, I expected that Black men in this book would resonate deeply with feelings of invisibility. However, while there were a few moments when a couple of the men resonated with the feeling of invisibility, they did not resonate with feelings of invisibility as much as they did with their experiences of being hyper-visible in American society. Throughout our conversations, they expressed that they feel very visible. In fact, they seem to interpret invisibility as a safe place where one is left alone as opposed to the hyper-visible moments of "being pointed at every second of my life." In this sense, they viewed invisibility as a state of peace. Contrasting the ways that White people are given the benefit of the doubt to be invisible versus the hypervisibility of Black people, Kendrick shared the following example:

> . . . it's a video I saw. A guy. . . . It's, I guess a state where you can walk around with an open carry. White guy walked down the street, M-16. Nobody says nothing. Cops [asked], "What are you doing?" [The white guy said] "Oh, I'm just walking my dog." Black guy does the same thing, [and the police said] "Get down on the ground." He's like [quoting the Black guy], "I got my credentials and everything. What are y'all doing?" So I mean, he wasn't invisible then.

Matthew described moments in his life when he wanted to be invisible. I asked him why he wanted to be invisible. He said, "Stealth. I like the stealth. I like being able to go into a space of peace. Invisibility to me, if I can frame it that way, is peace. It's a place of stillness. It's a place of quiet. It's a place I can go within myself or even in a room where I'm not being inundated by others' energies."

Eddie used the term invisibility to describe how Black men are not valued in the criminal justice and educational systems:

> But what about all the black people that's been killed? But the police have more life or more life is valued of a police officer. Or you can go to jail for ten years if you kill a police dog. You get hard time. But if the police kill you, they get off scot-free. So it's like being invisible is like: we're invisible to a certain point where we're not valued. But even in schools and education I've seen it where kids aren't valued or their opinions aren't valued, particularly black males. And schools are set up like prisons where in-school suspension is like solitary confinement for most kids, even for, particularly, black males.

Using the monster metaphor, we can gather that this is part of what it means to be "looked at" like a monster in the criminal justice system, school system, and society-at-large. Black men, as monsters, have less value than police dogs, police officers, non-Black students, and non-Black citizens.

Amidst the realities of being "looked at" through the lens of having less value than other humans and animals (in the case of the police dog), we need to remember that not all Black men embody the same views. Matthew's view about how he is looked at by others is slightly different than the aforementioned views articulated by Jamal, Darrell, and Eddie. It was as if Matthew did not want to acknowledge the negative aspects of Black male life. He also did not allow himself to be perceived as weak or vulnerable. When I asked Matthew to reflect on a time in his life when he felt devalued, he paused for ten seconds and responded,

> Hmm. I think you stumped me. That's a tough one. . . . I've always known that I was here to do something. I've always known. Um, that's a challenging question. I've seen people try to handle me a certain way, but I've never let that be the case. Even when I waited tables or even when I, anything that would be considered service-oriented, I've always carried myself with a level of, "I'm taking care of this person the same way I would want to be taken care of." So therefore I even still have value within myself where I don't feel subservient or feel like someone is greater than me. I always know when God uses me to provide value or bring insight to others. . . . So honestly, I can see how people try to deny acknowledgment to things or how they would attempt to try to make me feel devalued. But my, my belief and understanding my own foundations that has been instilled by my family has caused me not to even be affected by others in terms of devaluation. So that's really a challenging question for me because I could find the opposite in every situation and use that to draw from. I can't honestly say that I've ever felt a time of being devalued. If I ever felt an inkling of it, I would use that opportunity, "ok where do I find a solution?" I find something out of it.

On first read, we can observe that God and family enable Matthew to deflect the negative effects society would otherwise have on his life. God and family give him a sense of identity and purpose not dictated by the norms of a racist society. And yet if we listen deeply to Matthew's story, we can also observe that while he exudes tremendous energy to remain strong without being negatively affected by the potentially harmful racist gaze of society, he acknowledges that he has seen people try to treat him in three ways. First, he has seen people try to "handle [him] a certain way." Second, he has seen people try to "deny acknowledgment to things." Finally, he has seen people try to "make [him] feel devalued." In this sense, we can gather that he has felt the negative gaze on his life from others in his world, but has developed coping skills to deflect negative impacts on his psyche. While such a move can be viewed as commendable, I question whether or not one can live one's life without being affected by the racist ideologies and actions of the world in which one exists. This conversation will be taken up with greater depth in chapter six.

Ultimately, people fear and avoid monsters. This has been true for a growing number of Black men throughout this nation's history and continues in our contemporary times, as exemplified by the cases of police brutality against unarmed Black men. Police brutality is just one manifestation in which Black men are disregarded, disrespected, discredited, feared, and devalued. According to society, which abides by a White ideological norm, Black men, as monsters, do not exist as human beings. If we take seriously our monster analogy, we can note that people scream when they see monsters and cry out to a mother or father who has the power to eliminate the monster so that one can go back to sleep and rest. Because the monster is not human, the monster does not belong and is routinely looked at and treated as non-human. The monster must be controlled and eliminated by any means necessary. In similar fashion, society fears and avoids Black men. One can, therefore, determine that being "looked at" and treated as a monster is an inescapable reality for Black men living in the United States.

Questioned and Excluded from the Group

In addition to being "looked at like we're monsters," Black men have been frequently questioned and excluded from groups. Returning to the monster metaphor, we can begin to understand the dynamics of being questioned and excluded if we consider that monsters are not human and strike fear in the minds and bodies of people. Therefore, when a monster shows up and interacts with humans, the monster is immediately determined to be out of place. The monster is subsequently feared, questioned, and eliminated from the group so that all in the group can relax and continue living with feelings of peace and safety. Likewise, the men in this study reflected on experiences of being unjustly questioned and excluded from participation in groups. They have been alienated from society's rich well of resources and have not been welcomed to participate in groups that would, otherwise, provide Black men with resources to flourish. This move to alienate Black men from resources that would help one attain human flourishing is employed when those who have power and access to resources 1) question and exclude Black men from equal participation in society, and 2) deny Black men access to resources. Alienation in this regard has significant consequences in the lives of Black men. Perhaps the most obvious consequence in our contemporary culture is the images of police brutality against unarmed Black men who are fatally gunned down and choked in the streets of America. Yet, being questioned and excluded also has severe consequences for Black men beyond police brutality. An example of the severe consequences of being questioned and excluded include a Black man's experience on the job. The following narrative provides such an example. Kendrick recalled a time when he was questioned while working for his job. He notes,

> Perfect example. I was working for [my communications company]. . . . If I was a white guy with all this stuff on, walking in people's yard, they would not have said nothing. They called the police on me and this Puerto Rican guy. We got the [company] helmet, jacket, vest, everything on. And they like, "What are y'all doing?" [Kendrick responded]: "Working! Why you talking about 'what are we doing?'" So it's invisibility sometimes when they don't want to be bothered with you and then other times it's very noticeable and arrogant. I was just in a guy's house yesterday doing an installation, and he said how some people called and said, "This guy walking down the street." They pulled up on him and said, "Man, what's going on?" He said, "Man I just want to take a walk outside." Dude had a full pocket of money, everything. They just concerned. If it was a white guy, he would have been invisible.

Darrell also reflected on experiences of being questioned and excluded. He shared,

> Like if you walk in a room and you in this big room with these millionaires and everybody is talking about you because they like, "Why is he here? He not a rapper. I don't know him. He not an entertainer. What is he doing?" He's automatically getting questioned, because you're not in that realm. So it's just like, that's why I love it (being black), cuz I love that feeling. Like I'm not a rapper, but I'm in the same room as you. I love that feeling, but at the same time it makes it 100 times harder. . . . It's like playing Monopoly. Everybody starts negative and you only got one dice. White folks got two dice. They going quicker on the board. We only got one dice and the highest number is three.

In addition to Darrell sharing his experiences of being questioned by others, he also noted moments in his life when he was excluded from participation in groups while in school. He shared one of these moments in the following narrative:

I can tell you a lot of times. Like, it could just be just in class maybe in college. . . . [For] group projects. . . . I don't know what it just was. Didn't nobody know me. I didn't relate to anybody in my class. But I just felt like I wasn't of value to anybody in the group. I was always the guy that had to go to the teacher like, "I don't have no group." And so like it was another black girl named. . . . I remember her, she was in a couple of my classes and nobody wanted to pick her, cuz she was probably, you know, black. So it's me and her. We didn't have nobody, and then this big oversized obese white girl, and she wasn't well-liked cuz she kinda was urban a lil bit, so she didn't get picked either, so we formed a group. I feel like in the back of my head, in the back of everybody head in that group, you knew like we was like the (Darrell laughs) the foster kids group. We made it happen though.

Expected "to act a certain way"

The men in this book also acknowledged that people expect Black men "to act a certain way." Sharing an experience of a co-worker maintaining a particular expectation for Black people, Kendrick expressed:

I went to the Navy and I told one of the guys, "Yeah my entire student population at my school was black." And he couldn't believe that. He was like, "what do you mean?" I say, "the only white people there was teachers." [The other guy says]: "They can't do that." (*Kendrick & I laugh*). I said, "Ok man, this is Chicago. This is what they do." And he couldn't believe it. And then I threw him off just because of my name and how I acted. They said, "You don't act right." I said, "I know. I'm not the average black guy. I mean what do you think?" They just . . . they expected me to act a certain way and I didn't. I threw 'em off. I like that.

Kendrick's story provides an example of a Black man's co-worker expecting Black men "to act a certain way." Yet, when Kendrick's accomplishments and actions did not match their expectations of him, Kendrick's co-worker felt that he was not acting right. What does it mean for a Black man not to act right? It appears that "not acting right," according to Kendrick's White co-worker, is a phenomenon that occurs when a Black man deviates from the norms and expectations that a White-dominated society imagines for Black men. This form of limited expectation for Black men is yet another way that Black men are disregarded, disrespected, discredited, feared, and devalued. If internalized in Black male psyches, the negative and limited expectations society has of Black men has the potential to limit the world of possibilities imagined in their psyches. Hence, mental flourishing in this context means that the psyches of Black men must possess the strength, vision, tenacity, resolve, and resilience necessary to overcome negative external projections which do not promote life-giving possibilities for Black men.

RESPONSES TO BEING CHRONICALLY DISREGARDED, DISRESPECTED, DISCREDITED, FEARED, AND DEVALUED

How does one respond to daily experiences of being disregarded, disrespected, discredited, feared, and devalued? I was intrigued that each man in this book dealt with this social reality differently. While there were certainly similarities, each man dealt with society's negative blows to the psyche in his own unique way. The men in this book responded to society's negative blows to the psyche by: 1) meditating; 2) "prov[ing] them wrong" with positivity and intelligence; 3) presenting other life options for Black men; and 4) cutting people out of their lives. Additionally, a common sentiment among the men was a yearning for peace amidst a social reality of "being pointed at every second of my life" and "picked on" by society.

Meditation

In response to the question, *"So what do you do when you feel devalued?"*, Matthew expressed,

> The first thing I try to do, my form of meditation, is cycling. So, if it's something I feel like really kind of confused around or trying to understand like, "what was that all about?" I get on a bike and I ride. I do miles. And by the end of that cycle, I normally have an answer or perspective to that question that I posed. It gives me peace and the whole time I'm breathing in and out I'm exercising my soul as well. And, so, the particular act of devaluation or attack on the spirit has already been worked out. So, I'm able to process and breathe through it, and then come to a place of clarity of emotionless understanding, not one triggered by emotions. Well, all emotions is is energy in motion. So, if I'm controlling my energy properly, then I'm moving and manifesting my life in a clear and non-emotional way; which I think is the essential of it all. It gives me clarity. It gives me definiteness, purpose, and uh I normally cycle it out. And by the time I get to twenty miles or thirty miles, whatever everyone else's opinion is has no bearing on me.

Responding to the question, *"What do you do when you feel devalued?"*, Kendrick expressed: "What do I do when I feel devalued? I just uh . . . I reflect. I reflect and see why people treat me that way . . . cuz when people treat you differently that's because they don't know no better. They're going to devalue you." According to Matthew and Kendrick, meditation and reflection helped them to gain a better perspective on why they were devalued by others. In the case of Matthew, he explicitly said that meditation in the form of cycling brings him peace. Eddie said that he listens to music, reads, and writes to take a mental break:

Like I listen to a lot of music and just try not to flood my mind with negative thoughts or things that are gonna get me upset or like I know that I'm passionate about. I take a break, a mental break by reading. I read a lot. And I do a lot of writing cuz that clears my mind. It's like a stress relief, but I also love doing it though also. And then it helps me get out the frustration. I communicate better when I write . . . when I write, my message with my words gets across much better. So, it helps me to alleviate a lot of pressure that I'm feeling.

I asked Jamal how he responds to being devalued. He said,

Uh, I contemplate. Sometimes I think maybe, like I said, maybe I should be this way. Um, sometimes it gets me angry and, like I said, as being from where I'm from fighting is always a first instinct for me. Um, I may feel that way sometimes but then, like I said, I just think about real life. I think about consequences. I think about the things that could happen if I choose to do something as stupid as fight someone. I have responsibilities and I tend to look at those a lot stronger and just, you know. . . . So I think about a lot of things now that I'm older before I do them.

Proving them Wrong with Positivity and Intelligence

Another response of men in this book to chronic experiences of disregard, disrespect, discrediting, being feared and devalued was to prove the negative assumptions and limited expectations about Black men wrong using positivity and intelligence. Jamal uses positivity and intelligence as responses to his experiences of being "looked at" like a monster. He noted, "It's like be positive, but at the same time, not be a pushover. I feel that in ways that they can respectfully discredit us, we can respectfully discredit them too, or respectfully let them know that we're not idiots, you know. I guess in some ways kill 'em not with kindness but with intelligence." From Kendrick's perspective: "[People] assume all the time . . . I don't shoot people and do all that other stuff and gang bang and none of that. But they just make assumptions. . . . It's just it sucks that it's like that." As a response to these negative assumptions that others have of him, Kendrick expressed,

I just prove 'em wrong. I prove 'em wrong by acting how I act. That way, when they interact with me, they know that not all of [us] are the same. That's how I deal with it. There's no other way. I mean, I see it in the news and it's nothing I can do. But I mean I get frustrated, but you can only get frustrated for so long. Just be myself and not fall victim to their rules and stuff. . . . Like now, if somebody calls me a black . . . or a white person may say "nigga" to piss me off, I don't react how . . . I don't give them that reaction because that's what they want. So I don't do it. I just say, "ok you stupid," and walk off . . . They want us to react that way. If you don't give them that reaction, that throws them off and now they don't know how to react.

Presenting Other Life Options for Black Men

While society maintains limited expectations for Black men, the men in this book try to present other life options for other Black men. During an interview with Jamal, he expressed,

> Um, as I said, in certain conversations I try to bring up that there are other options. There are other ways; other things that we could be doing other than fighting for a block that we actually don't own. So, I mean those are some things that we probably need to stop doing. It just needs to be more of an understanding of other things that can be done with life. You know.

Toward the end of our first interview, he emphasized the importance of presenting other options to Black men:

> Like I said, once again I am being recorded, so I would love to just stress that as a black man let's do better. Let's learn other ways of communication with each other because, like I said, us killing each other ain't hurting nobody but ourselves, you know. There are other things than the block. There are other ways of enjoying life than seeing someone else hurt. That's it, pretty much.

Matthew also strives to share other life options with Black men by changing the narrative. He noted, "We are psychic leaders and so I teach that and I believe in that and seek to wake up every morning and remind myself of that. You know, so that's what it's about: Changing that narrative. Changing our story about how we see ourselves."

Cutting People Out

While much of the battle Black men face stems from the actions of White people who embrace and perpetuate White dominance against the flourishing of Black people, an additional battle Black men face concerns the ways that internalized racism affects Black people in the form of destructive relationship patterns amongst Blacks, as well as the ways that Black people have internalized an inferiority complex. The men in this book cope with this reality by cutting certain people out of their lives. Eddie shared, "[t]he other thing I've been doing to relieve stress is just cutting certain people out of my life. So that's another way to alleviate." He explained, "for the most part [I] just try not to associate myself with too much people that's doing negative things. They still my friends. I don't love them no less. But it's like they still at a point where they can't respect my opinion or how I feel. So I just try to find different people and different avenues." Kendrick noted that when it comes to people in his life who are not engaged in constructive behavior, he chooses not to come around much:

> If I look at majority of my friends that I grew up with now, they doing the same thing . . . They want more, but they're not doing anything to get to that point. They got goals, but they're being stagnant and just hoping for some mystery to happen; something mysterious to happen to get them there instead of working towards it. So, I don't come around a lot [Kendrick laughs]. Like, I'm more of an introvert. I don't hang out a lot with my friends cuz they don't inspire to do anything but chill out in the hood and get wasted. I mean that's fine, but every day? That's not what I'm trying to do. That's about it.

He later elaborated,

> I go around and show my face and talk to em, and then I be like, "Hey, y'all want to go play ball? Y'all want to go do something creative? Instead of just sitting around here to get drunk. [Kendrick pauses for two seconds]. Let's go play ball. Let's go do something constructive instead of . . ." But they don't see it. So I mean I come around it until they get on my nerves. It's time to go. It's just . . . I mean they don't say nothing about it. It's just, I got other priorities. Like, I'm active in my child's life where a lot of them ain't. They just sit out and get drunk all night. I mean that's fine, but I got a child to take care of to raise to be a man. So I can't be out there. I got to set the example and that's what I try to do.

In Kendrick's case, while there is an element of cutting his friends out of certain aspects of his life, he still tries to connect, but on a limited basis because he has a different vision for his life than his friends from childhood. From Kendrick's narrative, and the narratives of other Black men in this book, we get a sense of how they experience life and the ways that they respond to racism's impact on their lives and communities. Taking seriously the ways that Black men experience reality, and the ways that they make sense of their lives, positions those of us who care for Black men to care optimally for their lives.

INDIVIDUAL, INSTITUTIONAL, AND CULTURAL RACISM

Black psychology provides helpful resources for interpreting the psychological lives of Black people. Black psychology has explored the psychological impacts of systemic oppression, namely racism, on the lives of Black people in a way that helps us interpret the psychological lives of Black men. James Jones' chapter, "Race and Racism," in the book *African American Psychology: From Africa to America*, explores various types of racism impacting the psychological lives of Black people. Jones identifies three types of racism: individual, institutional, and cultural. "Individual-level racism is synonymous with racial prejudice. This type of racism assumes the superiority of one's own racial group and rationalizes the dominance and power generally of Whites over African Americans."[6] Further,

> Institutional racism is revealed by policies and practices within organizations and institutions that contribute to discrimination for a group of people. In this context, one does not have to be an individual racist in order for racism to occur in institutions. Institutional racism can also be thought of as structural or systemic racism that continually leads to adverse outcomes for African Americans . . . Cultural racism is seen in the assumed superiority of a language or dialect, values, beliefs, worldviews, and cultural artifacts dominant in a society. This racism is perhaps the most insidious of all in terms of identification and change because culture, by its nature, is institutionalized, with pervasive effects on all aspects of life.[7]

The narratives of the five men in this chapter provide concrete examples of the ways that Black men have experienced individual, institutional, and cultural racism. A keen awareness of the ways that Black men experience individual, institutional, and cultural racism will aid spiritual caregivers', mental health professionals', and community leaders' ability to care for the lives of Black men. Further, the work of those caring for Black men should include activism, community organizing, and political action so that individual, institutional, and cultural racism can be dismantled in society, enabling Black men to have greater opportunities to survive and flourish in the world.

CONCLUSION

In this chapter, we have explored the ways that Black men in this book have been chronically disrespected, disregarded, discredited, feared, and devalued. They experience life in this way daily because they are: *Not Known, "Looked at Like We're Monsters," Questioned and Excluded from the Group,* and *Expected "to Act a Certain Way."* These four subthemes take their cue from the manifestations of racism in society. While the negative social impacts on the psyches of Black men in this book were more similar than not, the specific ways in which each man dealt with this reality varied. They dealt with their experiences by: *meditating, "proving them wrong" with positivity and intelligence, "presenting other life options" for Black men,* and *"[cutting] people out."* The chapter concluded by naming three types of racism—individual, institutional, and cultural—identified by Black psychology as a way to understand the nuances of racism and its impact on the psychological lives of Black people. Understanding the negative social forces impacting the lives of Black men, and Black men's subsequent responses to these impacts, will aid our efforts to care optimally for the mental health of Black men.

NOTES

1. bell hooks, *We Real Cool: Black Men and Masculinity* (New York: Routledge, 2004), xi–xii.

2. All names are pseudonyms to protect the confidentiality of the research participants.

3. By using the word *chronically*, I am naming that the Black men in this book experience disregard, disrespect, discrediting, and are feared and devalued on a daily basis.

4. Faye Z. Belgrave and Kevin W. Allison, *African American Psychology: From Africa to America* (Thousand Oaks: Sage Publications, 2019), 114. This quote was offered in the context of reflections on a meta-analysis by Pieterse, Todd, Neville, and Carter (2012) that reviewed 66 studies which examined the links between mental health and racism. The sample size across the 66 studies totaled 18,140 people.

5. That is, if in fact a Black man is able to elude the criminal justice system and being fatally shot by the police.

6. Belgrave and Allison, *African American Psychology: From Africa to America*, 104.

7. Belgrave and Allison, *African American Psychology: From Africa to America*, 104–105.

Chapter Two

Breathing Racism's, Sexism's, and Classism's Toxic Air

To care adequately for the mental health of Black men, caregivers, mental health professionals, community leaders, and all persons caring for Black men need to develop and maintain an awareness of the ways that history and social context impact Black men. In this spirit, I have selected the work of several individuals to help us reflect on phenomena occurring in the lives of Black men interviewed in this book. We need a keen awareness of the cultures in which Black men exist to make possible opportunities for survival and flourishing. Attempts to care for the mental health of Black men, without awareness and acknowledgment of the cultural realities impacting Black men, are inadequate and, in fact, do more harm than good. Conversations with men in this book revealed that they were significantly impacted by the negative cultural images and expectations of Black men that are present in the United States and around the world. Similarly, they are affected daily by negative treatment from people in society who relate to Black men based on negative cultural images and expectations of Black men in the media and society. We can, therefore, affirm that cultural environments matter and have tremendous impact on the lives of Black men.

An everyday example may be helpful. I wear eye contact lenses. Occasionally, they cause my eyes discomfort. A few days ago, I drove to a local store to purchase new contact solution for my contacts. Upon my return home, I emptied the old contact solution from my contact lens case and poured in the new solution. I did not change the contacts, just the solution in which they sat. After shaking the contact lens case to clean my contact lenses in the new solution, I placed the contacts in my eyes. Immediately, the contacts rested in my eyes, giving me extreme comfort. The contacts were not the problem. The old dirty solution (its environment) was the problem.

The old dirty solution was polluted and needed to be replaced with new clean solution in order for my contact lenses to function properly. In other words, context matters.[1]

Similarly, the social contexts surrounding Black men in the United States often prevent Black men from surviving and flourishing as our optimal selves due to the cultural workings of racism and sexism.[2] Black men have faced this contextual reality since the beginning of our nation's history. Following the lead of Lee Butler, I assert that a psychohistorical approach is necessary to foster psychological liberation and healing in the lives of Black men. During a 2012 work-in-progress session at the Society for Pastoral Theology (SPT) study conference, Butler declared that a psychohistorical approach is necessary when developing theories of care and counseling. A Hope to Keep Going framework for care and counseling maintains a psychohistorical perspective on the lives of Black people living in the context of the United States.

Africans were ripped from their families and homeland beginning in 1441 at the start of the European slave trade. The first enslaved Africans arrived in the United States in 1619 in the city of Jamestown, Virginia. Slavery began in the United States in 1619 and, in theory, ended when Abraham Lincoln signed the Emancipation Proclamation in 1863. However, slavery did not officially end until the Thirteenth Amendment abolished slavery in 1865. After enslaved Africans became free citizens, America soon ushered in a new era of "separate but equal" through the court decision, *Plessy v. Ferguson*, in 1868. As a result, White Americans could enjoy the perceived comforts of living separately from the "Coloreds."[3] Even if a White person was poor, she or he could rest in the assurance that "at least I'm not a Negro." *Plessy v. Ferguson* mandated separation in public schools, drinking fountains, bathrooms, waiting areas, and other sites of public engagement. Meanwhile, Blacks lived without the necessary resources to survive and flourish and were lynched as Whites watched with pleasure, often capturing photos of the lynchings on postcards, which were sent to their White family members. Due to the United States' recognition that its treatment of Black people through lynchings, and particularly the separate but equal doctrine, was casting America in a negative light to its global partners, particularly countries such as India, the United States government moved to desegregate public schools in the *Brown vs. Board of Education* decision of 1954. Derrick Bell argues that Black suffering alone, however, is not what prompted America to desegregate public schools. Rather, Black people were fortuitous beneficiaries as America looked to strengthen its relationship with global partners. Even so, the perceived success for Black people was short-lived with the entrance of *Brown II* and the accompanying resistance to integration. The initial *Brown vs. Board of Education* decision to integrate schools did not necessarily prove advantageous for Black Americans. Likewise, historical inquiry reveals that the cultural environments in the United States have not been advantageous for the survival and flourishing of Black men. Our contemporary age of Black Lives Matter reveals that this is still the case. An honest look at our nation's history reveals that the United States of America maintains a bloody history of racial and gender oppression which has a negative impact on the contemporary cultural and intrapsychic experiences of Black men.

I address in this chapter the cultural contexts affecting the psyches of Black men and reference theorists who: 1) unpack the cultural workings of racism and sexism; 2) point to race as religious discourse; 3) critique Black machoism/male privilege; and 4) acknowledge intersubjective reality. I do so, first, by referencing critical race theorists Derrick Bell, Angela Harris, and Emma Jordan to unpack the material workings of racism. This is followed by a discussion of Stephen Ray's reflections concerning race as religious discourse. Third, I engage a critique of Black male machoism/male privilege as explicated by L'Heureux Lewis-McCoy, Michelle Wallace, and Chanequa Walker-Barnes. Finally, I discuss intersubjectivity from sociological and cultural perspectives by referencing the works of W. E. B. Du Bois and Katrina Bell-Jordan as an introductory investigation of the ways that racism and sexism impact the intersubjective experiences of Black men. By unpacking the deep-seated power of racism and sexism, I argue that to care optimally for the lives of Black men, racism and sexism need to be the starting point of our discussions of spiritual care, counseling, and community leadership.

CRITICAL RACE THEORY—CONTRIBUTIONS OF DERRICK BELL, ANGELA HARRIS, AND EMMA JORDAN

Derrick Bell, Angela Harris, and Emma Jordan provide helpful theoretical frameworks for understanding racism's sophistication and its material workings. I first turn attention to Derrick Bell, who argues that racism is permanent in society. His view of racism's permanence is a central tenet undergirding his theory on race. In the introduction, I pointed to the ways that, in spite of Black suffering, America chooses to keep going, passing Black men by without empathic concern. To this point, while Bell acknowledges that racial progress is ever changing, he notes that America continues to operate as a White country that does not extend resources and empathy to Blacks in ways extended to similar-situation Whites.[4] Bell's view on the possibilities for racial progress can be crystalized in the following statement:

> Black people will never gain full equality in this country. Even those herculean efforts we hail as successful will produce no more than temporary "peaks of progress," short-lived victories that slide into irrelevance as racial patterns adapt in ways that maintain white dominance. This is a hard-to-accept fact that

all history verifies. We must acknowledge it, not as a sign of submission, but as an act of ultimate defiance.[5]

Bell notes that "African Americans must confront and conquer the otherwise deadening reality of our permanent subordinate status. Only in this way can we prevent ourselves from being dragged down by society's racial hostility. Beyond survival lies the potential to perceive more clearly both a reason and the means for further struggle."[6] A goal, then, is to "fashion a philosophy that both matches the unique dangers we face, and enables us to recognize in those dangers opportunities for committed living and humane service."[7] Bell's theory, then, affirms that Black people will forever exist as subordinate citizens in the United States. However, Bell asserts that Black people can still survive and live a meaningful existence if we fully acknowledge the dangers we face and find "opportunities for committed living and humane service."[8] Thus, accepting racism as a permanent social construct in American and global society, Bell develops the concepts of racial-sacrifice covenants, interest-convergence covenants, and racial fortuity. These concepts, outlined in the next section, help us acknowledge the dangers facing Black people.

Racism's Sophistication

In his book, *Silent Covenants: Brown v. Board of Education and the Unfulfilled Hopes for Racial Reform,* Derrick Bell reflects on *Brown vs. Board of Education* and points out that while many praised the decision to integrate public schools as a sign of racial progress, "by doing nothing more than rewiring the rhetoric of equality, the *Brown* Court foreclosed the possibility of recognizing racism as a broadly shared cultural condition."[9] Identifying racism as a broadly shared cultural condition, Bell provides an explanation of racism's sophistication in his concepts of racial-sacrifice covenants, interest-convergence covenants, and racial fortuity.

Racial-Sacrifice Covenants

Bell observes that "[i]n Prehistoric Times, a people fearing that they had irritated their gods would seek to make amends by sacrificing a lamb, a goat, or sometimes a young virgin."[10] Sacrifices renewed connection between humans and the divine.[11] Drawing a parallel to rituals of sacrifice in the United States, Bell believes that a "similar though seldom recognized phenomenon has occurred throughout American racial history. To settle potentially costly differences between two opposing groups of whites, a compromise is effected that depends on the involuntary sacrifice of black rights or interests."[12] The lives of Black people, therefore, are sacrificed to renew connection between White people and the god of White supremacy. Thus, the rights and interests of Blacks are involuntarily sacrificed at will. According to Bell, the modern-day cultural norms and practices of sacrificing Blacks' rights and interests undergirds death penalty rulings, drug-penalty rules, and the denial of equal opportunities in education.[13] Bell observes that "those holding or seeking office sacrifice the right to just criminal prosecutions by refusing to amend drug and other criminal laws and procedures that result in severe sentences for nonviolent offenses, sentences that are disproportionately meted out to black men and women."[14] Consequently, no Black person can escape the dangers of racial-sacrifice covenants.

Interest-Convergence Covenants

In addition to racial-sacrifice covenants, Bell developed the related concept of interest-convergence covenants, which observes that Black people benefit from social change only when Whites sense an opportunity to satisfy their own self-interests (such as improving their social status, political relationships, and quality of life). Consequently, "Black rights are recognized and protected when and only so long as policymakers perceive that such advances will further interests that are their primary concern."[15] Pointing to events of the past to highlight the reality of interest-convergence covenants, Bell notes,

> Throughout the history of civil rights policies, even the most serious injustice suffered by blacks, including slavery, segregation, and patterns of murderous violence, have been insufficient, standing alone, to gain real relief from any branch of government. Rather, relief from racial discrimination has come only when policymakers recognize that such relief will provide a clear benefit for the nation or portions of the populace.[16]

Ultimately, Bell sees interest-convergence covenants and racial-sacrifice covenants as two sides of the same coin "with involuntary racial sacrifice on the one side and interest-convergent remedies on the other."[17]

Racial Fortuity

Bell's third major concept, racial fortuity, asserts that Blacks are only fortuitous beneficiaries of policy-making in law. Describing the intricacies of racial fortuity, Bell observes that it is similar to a contract-law concept in which "the third-party beneficiary"[18] emerges when "two parties . . . contract to provide goods or services to a third party."[19] In this sense, Blacks are the third-party beneficiary "in racial policy-making . . . [A]s far as the law is concerned, they are only 'incidental' or fortuitous beneficiaries. That is, white policymakers adopt racial policies that sacrifice black interests or recognize and provide relief for discrimination in accordance with their view of the fortuitous convergence of events."[20] According to Bell, White policy-makers are never motivated to change policies on the basis of remedying Black suffering alone. Rather, Whites have their own interests (and that of the nation) in mind in policy-making decisions. As a result, Bell argues that racial equality is more illusory than real, and asserts that a commitment to racial equality "leads us to confuse tactics with principles."[21] In other words, Blacks have, at times, embraced the right principles when striving for racial equality, but have, at times, embraced the wrong tactics in these strivings because of the illusory nature of racial equality. Contrary to pursuits of racial equality, Bell recommends activist strategies. According to Bell, activist strategies "can be planned that will recognize when the self-interests of both society and African Americans will probably be in accord."[22] Hence, maintaining an awareness of the self-interests of Whites and the larger U.S. society is critical for advancing the conditions of Black people in policy-making.

In summary, Derrick Bell contends that Blacks will forever exist as a subservient racial group in the United States. Yet, by facing this truth and the dangers therein, Black people can develop and embrace a philosophy for living which opens possibilities for a meaningful existence and participation in the world, despite the devastating cultural and political blows to the psyche which stem from society's commitment to the category of race and the workings of racism. A Hope to Keep Going framework for care and counseling does not affirm Black people as subservient, but acknowledges that Black people might exist in the minds of others as subservient. A Hope to Keep Going approach to care and counseling, therefore, acknowledges the cultural and institutional dangers facing Black people in the United States and throughout the world. Embracing Bell's theory on race enables caregivers and mental health professionals to develop new approaches to care and counseling which name accurately the challenges facing Black men. Such approaches to care and counseling equip Black men with resources to resist negative images and expectations of Black men in the media and society.

Racism's Impact on Law and Economics— Biases Masked in "Neutrality"

Having cited Bell's concepts of racial-sacrifice covenants, interest-convergence covenants, and racial fortuity, I turn attention to the ways that Angela Harris and Emma Jordan describe racism's influence on law and economics. Arguing against claims of neutrality and objectivity, Harris and Jordan note that there is a gap between two groups of legal scholars: 1) traditional law and economic scholars; and 2) legal scholars. They observe,

> On one hand, traditional law and economics scholars, like economists, are interested in questions of rational choice, efficiency, wealth maximization, and

production and transactions costs. On the other hand, legal scholars concerned with questions of identity, including race, gender and sexual orientation have focused their scholarly investigations on issues of subordination, identity, cultural context, and legal indeterminacy.[23]

Harris and Jordan express that, with few exceptions, the two groups do not engage in conversation with one another and, as a result, maintain "separate world views and separate, even antagonistic, operating assumptions about how to evaluate market phenomena."[24] Amidst the disconnect between these two groups, Harris and Jordan set out to "investigate the problems of the market domain with respect for both cultures."[25] While they find the perspective of economic scholars helpful with its focus on "scientific measurement and numerical representation of experience,"[26] their "vantage point as scholars who have been active in anti-subordination theory, however, also leads [them] to be attentive to questions of identity, culture, context, history, and dominance."[27] Their interest in anti-subordination theory and identity, culture, context, history, and dominance aligns well with a Hope to Keep Going framework for care and counseling.

Focusing on the impacts of subordination in law and economics, Harris and Jordan argue that claims of neutrality play a significant role in both traditional legal theory and traditional economic analysis.[28] Concerning law, Harris and Jordan observe that "[i]n their declarations of 'truth,' legal opinions are presented as objective, indifferent, and neutral . . . Similarly, the market is based on the notion that a willing buyer and a willing seller will participate in an arm's length transaction according to their preferences."[29] However, Harris and Jordan argue that due to factors tied to identity, culture, context, history, and dominance, legal opinions are neither objective nor neutral. In addition, due to these same factors, a buyer or seller may not be able to participate in economic transactions. An awareness of the effects of people in power (in law and economics) maintaining allegiances to ideologies of objectivity and neutrality will better aid caregivers who seek to care optimally for the lives of Black men.

Commitments to neutrality in law limit Black men's opportunities for justice in the criminal justice system by refusing to acknowledge and accept factors impacting the lives of Black men as relevant facts. Harris and Jordan recall that "[l]awyer and legal scholar Herbert Wechsler promoted constitutional interpretation based on neutral principles, not the immediate results of particular cases."[30] Consequently, there is no room to consider the impact of individual and group identities, cultures, contexts, histories, and systemic dominance on legal cases. However, lawyer and critical race theorist Patricia Williams "challenges the 'blind application of principles of neutrality.'"[31] She claims that "Blacks are the objects of a constitutional omission which has been incorporated into a theory of neutrality."[32] Harris and Jordan further observe that "[c]ourts use the law as a screen through which certain facts emerge as relevant while other facts are sifted out as irrelevant."[33] Therefore, courts have the power legally to dismiss relevant facts affecting the lives of Black people as irrelevant. As a result, using commitments to legal neutrality as the guiding principle, courts have the power to dismiss important contextual facts affecting the lives of Black men. Important factors that significantly influence the lives of Black men are easily dismissed when the law hides under the guise of legal neutrality and objectivity.

Countering norms of legal neutrality, critical race theorists have suggested and demonstrated that narrative can function as a powerful tool for including the experiences of Black people as relevant facts. The narratives of Black men in this book are offered, in part, as a way to offer counterstories and counterperspectives to challenge the oppressive stories and perspectives of Black men that are guided by the norms of White racial ideology. Harris and Jordan note that "[n]arratives, when subversive instead of hegemonic, use an individual story to reveal a collective wrong."[34] As such, the counterstories of Black people, as an outgroup in U.S. society, can challenge the ingroup's stories and claims of neutrality. Members of outgroups are able to use counterstories "as 1) a means of self-preservation and 2) a means of lessening their own subordination."[35] In *Storytelling for Oppositionists and Others: A Plea for Narrative*, Richard Delgado notes that "stories about oppression, about victimization, about one's own brutalization—far from deepening the despair of the oppressed, lead to healing, liberation, mental health."[36] Delgado, therefore, affirms storytelling as a helpful tool for cultivating healing, liberation, and mental health. Similarly, a Hope to Keep Going framework for care and counseling encourages Black men to tell their stories and to listen deeply to the stories of Black women as a way to nurture the survival, healing, liberation, and flourishing of Black men in a non-hegemonic fashion.

Crystallizing what might now be obvious, a Hope to Keep Going framework for care and counseling draws from critical race theory by placing the narratives of Black men in the center of conversation, along with those of Black women and other women of color, so that their narratives, and the systemic factors impacting their narratives, will be taken seriously as relevant facts in law, in economics, and in our theories and practices of care and counseling.

RACISM AS RELIGIOUS DISCOURSE

Racism's Grip on Social Reality

While Bell, Harris, and Jordan offer critical race perspectives that help us understand racism's sophistication and impact in the realms of law and economics, Stephen Ray integrates the perspectives of critical race theory and the theological discourse of Paul Tillich to interrogate race. He argues that the idea of race operates at the deepest level of human existence, that of meaning-making, which enables a person to invest her or his whole self to its cause. Accordingly, Ray advocates for approaching the construct of race as a religious discourse. By religious discourse, he means "an epistemological matrix which provides symbolic opportunities (linguistic and physical) to engage the deepest meaning of human existence; or, as Tillich might suggest, the 'depth' of every dimension of human existence."[37] Ray affirms that the category of race, as a social construct, holds power of universal validity for those abiding by its ideology.

Race as Example of the Demonic

Integrating reflections on the category of race with Tillich's view of the Demonic, Ray suggests that "the workings of race are a clear example of the Demonic in our midst."[38] He notes that the workings of race, as the Demonic, are alluring to its devotees because the Demonic has the tendency to inaccurately be identified as an "experience of the Holy."[39] Tillich defines the Demonic in this way:

> The only sufficient term I found was in the New Testament use of the "demonic," which is in the stories about Jesus: similar to being possessed. That means a force, under a force, which is stronger than the individual good will. . . . Of course I emphasized very much I don't mean it in a mythological sense—as little demons or a personal Satan running around the world—but I mean it as structures which are ambiguous, both to a certain extent creative, but ultimately destructive. . . . I had to find a term which covers the transpersonal power which takes hold of men and of society.[40]

Ray notes that there are "features of race as it has functioned in modernity that bare a stark resemblance to . . . the Demonic. Perhaps the most important is its persistence as a meaning-making category which is presumed to have revelatory power in relation to persons and communities."[41] Ray goes on to express that it is best to "understand [the Demonic] as a misidentification of the Holy, and an inappropriate response of investing oneself based upon that error. So, then for Tillich, the Demonic is yet a dimension of the Holy but one whose power of fascination inexorably leads to destruction."[42] By engaging Ray's view that race functions as a misidentification of the Holy, we can begin to understand the alluring power of the category of race and the ways that it calls people to invest their whole selves to its cause. Those who consciously and unconsciously devote themselves to the god of race invest their whole selves to its cause and, consequently, "place" Black people at the bottom of society's well,[43] with young Black men as the insoluble figments in their imagination.

Social Implications of the Category of Race

Ray is not only interested in engaging in an analysis of how individuals devote their whole selves to the category of race. Rather, he is also concerned with the social implications of such a devotion. Acknowledging the category of race's impact on social reality, Ray expresses that race structures "the very way bodies and the communities they constitute are received and 'placed' in the commonsense that characterizes a society."[44] The idea of placement is key to Ray's argument, and an important concept to consider when we think about the ways that Black men are "placed" in society. Ray notes that, "By 'placed' I mean the way that humans are structured into a given social according to the morphology of the bodies with which they exist."[45] Given the implications of how Black bodies are placed in society—often as the least valued members of the human race, if granted human status at all—theories and practices of care and counseling must take seriously the ways that Black men are placed in contemporary American society and the larger world.

BLACK MALE PRIVILEGE, BLACK MACHOISM, AND WOMANIST CRITIQUES

While racism places Black men in society as oppressed people, sexism places unreflective Black men as oppressors of women in society. L'Heureux Lewis-McCoy provides a critique of Black male privilege in alignment with the aforementioned view that Black men are both oppressed and oppressors. He explains that in order to improve conditions for Black men, women, and the community, Black male privilege must be critically engaged.[46] Reflecting on his undergraduate experiences at Morehouse College,[47] he recalls that Black male privilege was prevalent in his college environment and that it hampered the educational and activist achievements of his fellow Morehouse brothers. His Morehouse brothers would say, "'Come on man, I mean . . . you know we (black men) have more important things to deal with than sexism.'"[48] Lewis-McCoy observes that while this attitude was prevalent during his Morehouse experience, Black male privilege continues to be prevalent in the larger society, as demonstrated when gender-related issues are placed on the backburner of social agendas.[49] To change this reality, Lewis-McCoy argues that Black men, including himself, (and I include myself), need to interrogate the ways in which Black men function as both the oppressed and oppressors in society if communities expect to disrupt the cycles of community failure related to gender discrimination.[50]

It is fruitful to engage Lewis-McCoy's definition of Black male privilege. He defines Black male privilege as:

> a set of often overlooked and unearned gender-related advantages that centers the experience and concerns of black men to the exclusion of others in the black community, particularly women. Black male privilege is an incarnation of male privilege that operates within the strictures of the African-American community's norms and mores. [51]

He further notes that "Men's Studies scholars have argued that notions of manhood are fashioned in opposition to womanhood and across race and class lines, [and that] men are coerced to pursue notions of hegemonic masculinity which represent the often-unattainable marker of 'true manhood.'" [52] Lewis-McCoy points out that Black male privilege is not exclusive to heterosexual males. Rather, "Masculinity studies have shown that not all men benefit from privilege the same, but all men benefit from gender privilege." [53] One may ask how gender privilege, in the form of Black male privilege, can continue without serious interrogation. According to Lewis-McCoy, it continues because of "a need for status maintenance among black men and less about what we would call misogyny in the most classical sense—woman hating." [54] Ultimately, Lewis-McCoy calls for a confrontation of Black male privilege and a "renewed look at men and masculinities." [55]

Wallace's Critique of Patriarchal Culture

Like Lewis-McCoy's observation that gender reform has been excluded from Black social agendas, Michelle Wallace's critique of Black politics in the 1960s confronts masculine bias. In her book, *Black Macho and the Myth of the Superwoman*, originally published in 1979, Wallace "described how women remained marginalized by the patriarchal culture of Black Power and the ways in which a genuine female subjectivity was blocked by the traditional myths of black womanhood." [56] Wallace notes that *The Moynihan Report* highlighted and perpetuated the idea that a successful Black woman was the cause of Black family dysfunction. The report "said that the black man was not so much a victim of white institutional racism as he was of an abnormal family structure, its main feature being an employed black woman. This report did not *create* hostility. It merely helped to bring the hostility to the surface." [57] Wallace states that this report was not written for Black women. Rather, the report demonstrated that "[i]t was a man's world." [58] *The Moynihan Report*, in effect, opposed the flourishing of Black women and communicated that the mere existence of successful Black women threatened the well-being of Black men and Black families. According to Moynihan, the successful Black woman was the problem.

Standing firmly against *The Moynihan Report*, Wallace critiques the patriarchal norms of society, noting that it has abided by the rules of a "man's world," and recalls the attitudes of Black male political leaders when Shirley Chisholm became the first Black person to run for President of the United States as a major-party candidate. Chisholm was not only the first Black woman, but the first Black person to accomplish this feat. Despite Chisholm's groundbreaking presidential bid, the majority of Black male political leaders refused to support Chisholm's bid for the White House. For these Black male political leaders, "when it came to Shirley Chisholm, being black no longer came first at all. It turned out that what they really meant all along was that the black man came before the black woman. And not only did he come before her, he came before her to her own detriment."[59] Insomuch as the actions of the majority of Black men opposed the success of Chisholm and numerous other Black women, the social norms of the "man's world" continued.

Reflecting on relational dynamics, Wallace notes that little attention was given to how Black males and females related to one another.[60] Wallace concludes that as a result, Black men have been unintrospective and oppressive toward Black women.[61] According to Wallace, Black men did not voluntarily become introspective about their dominant and oppressive views and actions toward Black women. A Hope to Keep Going framework for care and counseling challenges dominant and oppressive ways of relating and calls for Black men to be introspective about the ways that Black men view and interact with Black women. This is critical because, as Wallace notes, Black men maintained the view that they didn't owe Black women anything because—according to Black men—Black women sold out Black men and were already ahead of Black men in society.[62] This view, however, is inconsistent with the communal spirit of Ubuntu affirmed in a Hope to Keep Going framework for care and counseling. Black men who embrace the view—that Black men don't owe Black women anything—fuel divisions and unhealthy ways of relating between Black women and Black men. Likewise, Black men who embrace this view cannot flourish because this view does not nurture the survival and flourishing of Black women.

Wallace acknowledges a counter-argument to her position which asserts that Black men need support from Black women because White men have attempted to emasculate Black men and, in so doing, declared "you are not a man." As a result, internalized oppression manifested itself in the psyches of Black men. An aim of a Black man has since been to prove that he, in fact, is a man. Thus, Black men and women began to resent one another. As Wallace notes, "Only as American blacks began to accept the standards for family life, as well as for manhood and womanhood embraced by American whites, did black men and women begin to resent one another."[63] Black Americans began to accept the norms of White family life as the model after which to pattern their own lives. This practice of accepting White culture and nuclear families as the standard for Blacks effectively devalued Black life. In so doing, when Black men and women fell short of the White American ideal for manhood and womanhood in regard to wealth, social power, and standard of beauty, Black men and women resented one another.

Reflecting on the implications of Black men's lack of power and failed attempts to attain a White male standard of living, Wallace notes that the "Americanized black man's reaction to his inability to earn enough to support his family, his 'impotence,' his lack of concrete power, was to vent his resentment on the person in this society who could do least about it—his woman."[64] Hence, Black men treated Black women as objects and used them to release their frustrations with the world. We can, therefore, assert that because Black men have been unfairly granted social privileges not afforded to Black women, the consequences of racism are more severe to the well-being of Black women than to Black men. This means that we must place a critique of Black male privilege, or better yet, Black machoism, at the starting point of our conversations on the mental health of Black men so that Black women flourish as we cultivate opportunities for the flourishing of Black men.

While Wallace does not explicitly raise the perspectives of LGBTQ relationships and family bonds, serious consideration needs to be given to the ways that Black male privilege and machoism impact Black LGBTQ relationships. It is important to consider how facets of LGBTQ life impact Black romantic relations and family life. While it is beyond the scope of this book to explore more fully such dynamics with the depth that they deserve, I hope that by raising this important dimension of human experience the experiences of Black LGBTQ people will be taken seriously in our scholarly, clinical, and community dialogues.

Liberating Black Women from the Burden of Strength

We have so far explored Lewis-McCoy's and Wallace's contributions, which: 1) name Black male privilege as problematic; 2) advocate for introspection and a critique of patriarchal norms in our conceptions of Black masculinity, relationships between men and women, and social life; and 3) advocate for the advancement of Black women and explicit inclusion of their perspectives as a central dimension of our social agendas. Having explored these contributions, it is fitting to move toward reflection on a specific dimension of Black women's experience raised by Chanequa Walker-Barnes.

I am suggesting that theories of spiritual care, counseling, and community leadership explicitly consider Black women's burden of strength as a starting point of discussion on the care of Black men. To this end, it is helpful to explore Chanequa Walker-Barnes' work that expounds upon Black women's burden of strength and her concept of the twenty-first century StrongBlack-Woman. As a point of reference, she notes that the ideological ancestor of the StrongBlackWoman is the Superwoman named in Michele Wallace's book, *Black Macho and the Myth of the Superwoman.*[65]

In *Too Heavy a Yoke: Black Women and the Burden of Strength*, Walker-Barnes sparks "awareness and discourse about the inordinate burden that the demand for *strength* places upon women of African descent."[66] She observes that "[t]he StrongBlackWoman is not the problem, but is a symptom of a larger problem."[67] Walker-Barnes is, therefore, concerned with "cultivating practices of transformation that liberate Black women from the burden of strength."[68] Walker-Barnes explains that it "is certainly the case that an individual can be strong, black, and a woman without being the 'Strong-BlackWoman.' Yet, the societal pressure to be strong is so intense for Black women that many, if not most, embody at least some aspect of the Strong-BlackWoman at some point in their lives."[69] She identifies three primary markers of the StrongBlackWoman: 1) Emotional strength/regulation *(A STRONG Sista)*; 2) Caregiving *(The Consummate Caregiver)*; and 3) Independence *(Miss Independent)*.[70] Walker-Barnes notes that the StrongBlack-Woman has a trace of each of these primary markers to an excessive degree, which make them detrimental to a Black woman's health.[71] She notes that "Black women in the United States are experiencing epidemic rates of medical conditions such as obesity, diabetes, hypertension, and HIV/AIDS, and higher mortality rates for nearly every major cause of death than any other racial/ethnic group."[72] One can recognize the need for Black women to be liberated from the burden of strength when one realizes that "the Strong-BlackWoman forces upon African-American women unrealistic expectations for emotional strength and regulation, caring for others at the expense of one's own needs, and radical self-sufficiency, which in turn increase stress, role strain, and poor self-care behaviors."[73] Consequently, I am arguing that Black men must be attuned to the realities of the StrongBlackWoman and journey with Black women to help liberate them from the burden of strength by developing and embracing concepts of masculinity which care deeply for the lives of Black women.

Having explored the contributions of Lewis-McCoy, Michelle Wallace, and Chanequa Walker-Barnes, we can imagine new conceptions of Black masculinities capable of resisting racism, sexism, and Black machoism. In this sense, a Hope to Keep Going framework for care and counseling advocates for theories and practices of spiritual care, counseling, and community leadership with Black men to foster intentionally in Black men character traits that will: 1) help ensure Black women have opportunities to succeed as leaders in society; 2) refrain from embracing ideologies that encourage Black men to treat women as subservient people who exist solely for the purposes of pleasing Black men; and 3) embody deep listening, empathy, and support for the lives of Black women.

In this chapter, I have used the work of Stephen Ray to give religious/ theological language to the category of race, for an understanding of how individuals can give their whole selves to the cause of race/racism, and to acknowledge that Black people are placed in society in particular ways due to commitments to the category of race in modernity. I have also used the social scientific perspectives of Derrick Bell, Angela Harris, Emma Jordan, L'Heureux Lewis-McCoy, Michelle Wallace, and Chanequa Walker-Barnes to unpack the cultural workings of racism and sexism. The aforementioned authors describe what's happening socially and provide a way of engaging intersubjective reality in the particular contexts in which Black men live. The next section will help us think about these dynamics through the lens of W. E. B. Du Bois.

INTERSUBJECTIVE REALITY

Acknowledging intersubjectivity as a significant dimension of human experience can help us see that conversations on Black men's mental health should not be divorced from conversations on the realities of the social environments in which we live. This means that it is critical to maintain an awareness of the ways that racism, sexism, classism, heteronormativity, and other hegemonic forces have an impact on the psyches of Black men. An intersubjective approach to the care of Black men recognizes the impact of culture, history, family, co-workers, and other societal forces on the psyches of Black men.

"How Does it Feel to Be a Problem?"

W. E. B. Du Bois points out the implications of intersubjectivity for Black people by considering internal feelings in the context of social reality. As a Black person, Du Bois observes, "Between me and the other world there is ever an unasked question . . ."[74] For Du Bois, the unasked question is "*How does it feel to be a problem?*", which is posed in his 1903 publication *The Souls of Black Folk*. He notes that "being a problem is a strange experience— peculiar even for one who has never been anything else . . ."[75] To cope with the strange experience of being a problem, Black people develop a double-consciousness. Du Bois explains that double-consciousness is a "sense of always looking at one's self through the eyes of others, of measuring one's soul by the tape of a world that looks on in amused contempt and pity. One ever feels his two-ness—an American, a Negro."[76]

Du Bois also brings our attention to a specific dimension of social reality effecting Black life: the criminalization of Black men and the role police have historically played in policing, and ultimately controlling, Black men. Although written in the early 1900s, Du Bois' reflections help us see striking resemblances between the criminalization of Black men and the role police played in policing Black men in the early 1900s and the practices of police brutality that occur in our modern age of Black Lives Matter. Du Bois notes that "the political status of the Negro in the South is closely connected with the question of Negro crime."[77] He observes that "we must note two things: 1) that the inevitable result of Emancipation was to increase crime and criminals, and 2) that the police system of the South was primarily designed to control slaves."[78] Consequently, care of the mental health of Black men must include serious reflection on social context in the United States, a social context that often criminalizes Black men's very existence. Du Bois further notes that

> the police system of the South was originally designed to keep track of all Negroes, not simply of criminals; and when the Negroes were freed and the whole South was convinced of the impossibility of free Negro labor, the first and almost universal devise was to use the courts as a means of reenslaving the blacks. It was not then a question of crime, but rather one of color, that settled a man's conviction on almost any charge.[79]

Using the insights of Du Bois, I'm pointing to a generalized feeling among Black men that most of the people in our world look at us as if we are a problem. Reflection on this aspect of Du Bois' thought can help us understand how Black men experience the world. Admittedly, this reflection does not name how Black men participate in society. Black men's participation in society is a significant aspect of flourishing according to a Hope to Keep Going framework for care and counseling. In other words, Black men don't just receive what happens to them, but they have agency to participate in the world in meaningful and life-giving ways. It is critical for Black men to reflect on the ways that we (as I include myself in this discussion) participate in the world. Nonetheless, Black men's experience in the world (how we are related to) affects how we participate in it.

The Media Impacting Black Men

It is also helpful to consider the ways that contemporary culture affects Black men. Katrina Bell-Jordan helps us in this regard by observing that "contemporary culture continues to signify black masculinity as violent, sexual, criminal, and incompetent or uneducated; media perpetuate the hegemonic nature of racial images; and society continues to fear black men."[80] She recalls that,

> Chuck D., outspoken social and political activist (and founder of the group Public Enemy), says that African Americans: *"don't control our economics or*

education, our enforcement or our environment. Then there's the tendency of not having control over the realities, and that means the fantasy world can be dealt and sold to us very easily. So people become what they see, and when people become what they see, a reflection or a limited reflection can end up as a direct interpretation."[81]

In line with this thought, Herman Gray contends that,

> Like their jazz predecessors, contemporary expressions of [B]lack masculinity work symbolically in a number of directions at once: they challenge and disturb racial and class constructions of [B]lackness; they also rewrite and reinscribe the patriarchal and heterosexual basis of masculine privilege (and domination) based on gender and sexuality.[82]

Highlighting masculine privilege and domination, Bell-Jordan writes that "the tendency in hip hop to define black womanhood in opposition of black manhood has been problematized by critics for its 'blatant espousing of negative and destructive attitudes toward women', and for its use of language that demeans black women."[83] Bell-Jordan thus concludes that "representations [in hip-hop music and popular magazines] limit our understandings of the interests, abilities, occupations and depth of black males and their lived experiences in contemporary culture."[84] We can go a step further in suggesting that a significant dimension of Black men's experience in the world—their representations in hip-hop music and popular magazines—affects how Black men participate in the world. Each Black man deals with representations of themselves in hip-hop music and popular music differently. Yet, Black male representation in hip-hop music and popular magazines have an impact on the psyches of Black men, consciously and unconsciously. Representations of Black men in hip-hop music and popular magazines also impact the ways that people relate to Black men. In other words, even if a person does not regularly interact with a Black man, she or he can imagine and treat Black men in ways that seem fitting for the Black men represented in hip-hop music and popular magazines. We can therefore conceive that to care for the mental health of Black men, we must also care for the worlds in which we live, namely that of institutions and the media (including hip-hop music and popular magazines).

The work of the theorists in this chapter illustrate ways to think about racism, sexism, and classism in society and their impact on Black men. If one possesses a keen awareness of how one is placed in the social world, one is better able to discern strategic opportunities to participate in the world in ways that lead to the survival, liberation, healing, and flourishing. Black men must first be aware of how we experience the world before we can participate in it in meaningful ways so that we can creatively nurture our own survival, liberation, healing, and flourishing in the presence of life-giving community.

NOTES

1. It is worth noting that there are moments when the contact lens is damaged. Consequently, we can observe that the source of the problem (or, for our purposes, pathology) can be found in the contact solution and the contact lens. That is, to make the metaphor clear, context *and* intrapsychic experience are important and must be tended to in order to optimally foster human flourishing in the lives of Black men.

2. Sexism negatively compromises Black male identity by basing it on privilege over and against women. For the purposes of this book, I am particularly concerned with how Black male identity is conceptualized to perpetuate and maintain privilege over and against Black women.

3. When one thinks of color, it becomes apparent that white is a color, too. However, the nature of White privilege has been such that Whites can name all others "people of color" without acknowledging their own subjective position as people of color.

4. Derrick Bell, *Silent Covenants: Brown v. Board of Education and the Unfulfilled Hopes for Racial Reform* (New York: Oxford University Press, 2004), 195.

5. Bell, *Faces at the Bottom of the Well: The Permanence of Racism* (New York: Basic Books, 1992), 12.

6. Bell, *Faces at the Bottom of the Well,* 12.

7. Bell, *Faces at the Bottom of the Well,* 195.

8. Bell, *Faces at the Bottom of the Well,* 195.

9. Bell, *Silent Covenants,* 197.

10. Bell, *Silent Covenants,* 29.

11. Bell, *Silent Covenants,* 29.

12. Bell, *Silent Covenants,* 29.

13. Bell, *Silent Covenants,* 29.

14. Bell, *Silent Covenants,* 44.

15. Bell, *Silent Covenants,* 49.

16. Bell, *Silent Covenants,* 49.

17. Bell, *Silent Covenants,* 69.

18. Bell, *Silent Covenants,* 69.

19. Bell, *Silent Covenants,* 69.

20. Bell, *Silent Covenants,* 70.

21. Bell, *Silent Covenants,* 189.

22. Bell, *Silent Covenants,* 190.

23. Angela Harris and Emma Jordan, *Economic Justice: Race, Gender, Identity and Economics* (New York: Foundation Press, 2005), 1.

24. Harris and Jordan, *Economic Justice,* 1.

25. Harris and Jordan, *Economic Justice,* 1.

26. Harris and Jordan, *Economic Justice,* 1.

27. Harris and Jordan, *Economic Justice,* 1.

28. Harris and Jordan, *Economic Justice,* 2.

29. Harris and Jordan, *Economic Justice,* 7–8.

30. Harris and Jordan, *Economic Justice,* 8.

31. Harris and Jordan, *Economic Justice,* 9.

32. Harris and Jordan, *Economic Justice,* 9.

33. Harris and Jordan, *Economic Justice,* 9.

34. Harris and Jordan, *Economic Justice,* 11.

35. Harris and Jordan, *Economic Justice,* 12.

36. Harris and Jordan, *Economic Justice,* 12.

37. Stephen Ray, "An Unintended Conversation Partner: Tillich's Account of the Demonic and Critical Race Theory," 3.

38. Ray, "An Unintended Conversation Partner," 12.

39. Ray, "An Unintended Conversation Partner," 15.

40. Paul Tillich, "Paul Tillich and Carl Rogers: A Dialogue." Transcript of Video Interview (San Diego State, 1965), 69.

41. Ray, "An Unintended Conversation Partner," 12.

42. Ray, "An Unintended Conversation Partner," 9.

43. Here I am pointing to Derrick Bell's *Faces at the Bottom of the Well: The Permanence of Racism* (New York: Basic Books, 1992).

44. Ray, "An Unintended Conversation Partner," 8.

45. Ray, "An Unintended Conversation Partner," 8.

46. Brittany Slatton and Kamesha Spates, eds., *Hyper Sexual, Hyper Masculine? Gender, Race and Sexuality in the Identities of Contemporary Black Men* (New York: Routledge, 2014), 75.

47. Morehouse is an all-male Historically Black College in Atlanta, GA.

48. Slatton and Spates, eds., *Hyper Sexual, Hyper Masculine?*, 75.

49. Slatton and Spates, eds., *Hyper Sexual, Hyper Masculine?*, 76.

50. Slatton and Spates, eds., *Hyper Sexual, Hyper Masculine?*, 77.

51. Slatton and Spates, eds., *Hyper Sexual, Hyper Masculine?*, 77.

52. Slatton and Spates, eds., *Hyper Sexual, Hyper Masculine?*, 78.

53. Slatton and Spates, eds., *Hyper Sexual, Hyper Masculine?*, 78.

54. Slatton and Spates, eds., *Hyper Sexual, Hyper Masculine?*, 79.

55. Slatton and Spates, eds., *Hyper Sexual, Hyper Masculine?*, 83.

56. Michele Wallace, *Black Macho and the Myth of the Superwoman* (New York: Verso, 1999), back cover.

57. Wallace, *Black Macho and the Myth of the Superwoman,* 12.

58. Wallace, *Black Macho and the Myth of the Superwoman,* 12.

59. Wallace, *Black Macho and the Myth of the Superwoman,* 29.

60. Wallace, *Black Macho and the Myth of the Superwoman,* 13.

61. Wallace, *Black Macho and the Myth of the Superwoman,* 13.

62. Wallace, *Black Macho and the Myth of the Superwoman,* 19.

63. Wallace, *Black Macho and the Myth of the Superwoman,* 24.

64. Wallace, *Black Macho and the Myth of the Superwoman,* 24.

65. Walker-Barnes, *Too Heavy a Yoke: Black Women and the Burden of Strength* (Eugene: Cascade Books, 2014), 6.

66. Walker-Barnes, *Too Heavy a Yoke,* 8.

67. Walker-Barnes, *Too Heavy a Yoke,* 9.

68. Walker-Barnes, *Too Heavy a Yoke,* 10.

69. Walker-Barnes, *Too Heavy a Yoke,* 15.

70. Walker-Barnes, *Too Heavy a Yoke,* 18.

71. Walker-Barnes, *Too Heavy a Yoke,* 18.

72. Walker-Barnes, *Too Heavy a Yoke,* 44.

73. Walker-Barnes, *Too Heavy a Yoke,* 160.

74. W. E. B. Du Bois, *The Souls of Black Folk* (New York: Barnes & Nobles Classics, 2005 [original 1903]), 7.

75. Du Bois, *The Souls of Black Folk,* 8.

76. Du Bois, *The Souls of Black Folk,* 9.

77. Du Bois, *The Souls of Black Folk,* 126.

78. Du Bois, *The Souls of Black Folk,* 126.

79. Du Bois, *The Souls of Black Folk,* 127.

80. Bell-Jordan, Katrina. *Masculinity in the Black Imagination: Politics of Communicating Race and Manhood.* ed. Ronald Jackson and Mark Hopson (New York: Peter Lang, 2011), 129.

81. Bell-Jordan, *Masculinity in the Black Imagination,* 130.

82. Bell-Jordan, *Masculinity in the Black Imagination,* 132.

83. Bell-Jordan, *Masculinity in the Black Imagination,* 133.

84. Bell-Jordan, *Masculinity in the Black Imagination,* 135.

Chapter Three

The Urgency for Men to Embody Empathy and Support for Women

Chapter 1 highlighted racism's impact on the lives of Black men. I enlisted their narratives to demonstrate how racism in American culture affects the psyches of Black men living in the United States. Additionally, the narratives displayed how Black men mentally process daily experiences of being disregarded, disrespected, discredited, feared, and devalued. Drawing upon their stories, this chapter reflects on sexism's impact on Black male identity in relation to women. This chapter engages two primary questions from the purview of Black men: *How do I understand my identity as a man?* and *How do I participate in the world in relation to women?* Four subthemes, drawn from the data, can help us address these questions: The subthemes are: *1) Identifying men as providers and protectors; 2) Lacking empathy for the experiences of women; 3) Appreciating women for the pleasure women bring to men*; and *4) Identifying women as motherly, loving, caring, and understanding.* Each of these subthemes relates to one another and should not be viewed in isolation. Each subtheme has the potential to advance the hegemonic legacies of Black male identity, which are in opposition to the flourishing of women. My position here is that Black men cannot flourish without developing and maintaining empathy and support for the experiences and ambitions of women so that both Black men and women can flourish. bell hooks makes a similar claim when she states that "black males do need to practice empathy"[1] toward Black women. Living in solidarity with the experiences of women is a necessary component of Black male flourishing. Additionally, bell hooks calls on Black men to develop anti-patriarchal visions of Black masculinity, noting that there needs to be additional literature on this topic: "There is not even a small body of anti-patriarchal literature speaking directly to black males about what they can do to educate themselves for

59

critical consciousness, guiding them on the path of liberation."[2] She suggests that Black men must listen to Black women to become liberated from patriarchal visions of Black masculinity: "Listening to healthy emotionally mature black females is essential to black male self-recovery. . . . Listening to and learning from progressive black women is one way for black men to begin the work of self-recovery."[3] This book is an effort to add to the scant body of anti-patriarchal literature on the psychological and spiritual well-being of Black men. The pages in this chapter are offered as a way to critique patriarchal embodiments of Black masculinity in order to make possible opportunities for liberated Black male identities, which foster the survival, liberation, healing, and flourishing of women.

IDENTIFYING MEN AS PROVIDERS AND PROTECTORS

I first invite us to consider how Black men in this book understand their own masculine identity. They believe that being a provider and protector are key markers of masculinity. A few examples will be helpful. Kendrick responded to the question, "*What does it mean to be a man?*" by expressing,

> you have to give that light that you're a protector, regardless whoever is in your presence. Like I gotta let my son know, "don't worry about nothing. Daddy's here to protect you." If you less than a man, then you don't do stuff; like don't take care of your children or your responsibilities . . . people who I don't consider men don't care where they live at, don't care what they doing, don't care about nothing; whereas if you're a man you care about certain things because you want more. Most people want more. Especially being a man you want to have more because you want to be able to show it; that I can protect you, I'm a father. Cuz that's what women look at. Women look at, "Can he provide for me? Can he protect me?" And if you not, then you not really considered a man. That's how I look at it.

Responding to the same question, "*What does it mean to be a man?*," Matthew responded,

> To me, a provider. A rock. A lover. Uh, a sense of stability. Uh, an emotional bridge, one that can help create understanding about some of life's challenges, and you know the person who's supposed to be able to weather the storm of emotionality. . . . So, to me a man is a rock. A pillar of the community, someone who should teach not only his own children biologically, but also the children of the community. So it should be a father, if you will, father-figure for those who don't have a father as well. So I just feel like all of that falls under the authority of manhood.

Reflecting on the nature of women, Matthew articulated that a woman is "something that should be protected and cared for."

Speaking on what it means to be a man, Darrell expressed,

> Um, I feel like a man is a provider. Um, as far as a boy versus a man, I feel a man is more serious, like it's a more serious role. He takes care of his family; provides for his family. . . . My general idea of a man is a family man, a family-oriented man. A guy that takes care and is a man of his word. Like that's a man. Yeah, that's just what it is.

Responding to the question, *"What it means to be a man?,"* Eddie expressed,

> Oooh that's a complex question. I would say it goes back to different relationships you have with men in your life. . . . I was one of the cases where I didn't have my father in the household. But there aren't a lot of black male educators or administrators in public schools or even now with charter or private schools you don't see a lot of black males in that dynamic. So, the perception that's given to most black boys of what manhood is is the guy on the street corner that's a thug. . . . Like you don't want to show too much emotion, cuz then you seen as soft. . . . How you define manhood depends on the man. I would define manhood . . . well Malcolm X defined manhood as being a provider and protector of your family.

Three observations from the narratives above can help us unpack the notion of Black men as providers and protectors. First, there are positive and negative dimensions to a Black male functioning as a provider. Second, that which is modeled before Black men affects how a Black man comes to understand his role and function in relationship to women. Third, the expectations that women have of Black men affect the ways Black men see themselves.

To the first point, there can be positive elements to a Black man's functioning as a provider and protector. This includes taking responsibility so that his identity is not centered on selfish ambitions. The positive elements of a Black man's functioning as a provider and protector means that he is concerned with the well-being of others. Concern for the well-being of others positions Black men to maintain desire to help provide for the needs of others and protect others from harm. The men in this book imply that there are Black men who do not take care of their responsibilities. In this sense, Black men should be responsible to the women and children in their lives. I should also note that the Black men in this book did not explicitly state that it is important to provide for and protect other Black men. If Black men embrace the roles of providing for and protecting women and children, I suggest that Black men should also be concerned with providing for and protecting other Black men. Perhaps providing for and protecting women and children is more about maintaining one's own power and privilege more than a genuine interest in caring for the others. However, when one embraces a liberative approach to providing and protecting, the action is more about genuine care for the other than about maintaining one's own position of power and privilege. With this type of embrace, Black men might be able to provide for and protect other Black men out of a desire to embody empathy and care for the other. Ultimately, while Black men functioning as providers and protectors may, in moments, produce positive outcomes, the identity of Black men should not be tied solely to these two attributes because an over-identification with the notion of Black men as providers and protectors marginalizes other ways of being in authentic relationship with women and other men.

There are negative dimensions to understanding one's identity solely from the position of provider and protector. Such an identity affirms that "I cannot be weak, but must always be strong to provide and protect." This character trait can be detrimental to and taxing on Black men's mental health. I am thinking of Walker-Barnes' concept of "Too Heavy a Yoke." Walker-Barnes writes about the experiences of Black women. And, there are implications for the emotional health of Black men when we consider her notion of the consequences of carrying a heavy yoke. Here, we should note that Black men unfairly benefit from gender privilege and as such the yoke carried by Black woman is heavier than that carried by Black men. Thus, as we engage the implications of Walker-Barnes' work on the lives of Black men, we should not lose sight of how gender privilege affects Black women in ways distinct from Black men. I find Walker-Barnes' reflections on the consequences of carrying a heavy load beneficial for our discussion on the ways that Black men seek to remain strong at all costs. Black men carry heavy yokes when we understand our identities solely from the perspective of being a provider and protector. Such an identity is also oppressive to women because there are capable women who can also provide and protect. Additionally, an identity understood only in terms of providing and protecting gives Black men an excuse to not be in authentic relationship with women. It's as if, as long as I provide for you and protect you, I do not need to be in an authentically caring relationship with you.

To the second point, the model of Black masculinity in one's personal life impacts one's concept of Black male identity. As Eddie mentioned, "it goes back to different relationships you had with men in your life." In my role as therapist, I'm reminded of the significant impact that a male client's uncles had on his life, especially the ways that he learned to embrace his own Black male identity. His uncles engaged in sexual and romantic relationships with multiple women at once. Therefore, he, too, believed that such a lifestyle was normal and embraced it for his own life without being fully aware of how his actions caused emotional hurt to his girlfriend, who desired to be in a monogamous relationship. While this client was not a part of the empirical research study, he confirms Eddie's observation that relationships men have with other men affect a Black man's concept of masculinity. In addition to personal relationships with other Black men, Eddie demonstrates that key leaders in American culture affect Black men's understanding of manhood. Eddie expressed, "I would define manhood . . . well, Malcolm X defined manhood as being a provider and protector of your family."

To the third point, women's expectations of Black men can affect one's concept of Black masculinity. In the words of Kendrick, "Women look at, 'Can he provide for me?'. . . If not, you not considered a man." In this sense, the expectations women have of men matter. On the level of cultural reflection, we can consider, what do women expect from men? This question deserves greater attention than the delimitations of this book allows. Nonetheless, it is critical to reflect on the aspects of manhood that women accept beyond a Black male's role of provider and protector. Black men are aware of how society and, particularly, women view Black men. If we accept intersubjectivity as an inescapable dimension of human reality, then spiritual caregivers, therapists, and community leaders need to reflect on the images of Black masculinity embraced and accepted by women. This is part of the cultural milieu existing in the psyches of Black men.

There are multiple dimensions to Black men functioning primarily as provider and protector. I argue that an over-identification with the attributes of provider and protector prevents Black men from engaging in authentic and empathic relationships with women.[4] bell hooks argues that Black men had to learn how to identify the marks of providing and protecting as the hallmarks of masculinity from White slave masters during slavery. She states that

> enslaved black males were socialized by white folks to believe that they should endeavor to become patriarchs by seeking to attain the freedom to provide and protect for black women, to be benevolent patriarchs . . . it was this notion of patriarchy that educated black men coming from slavery into freedom sought to mimic . . . Clearly, by the time slavery ended[,] patriarchal masculinity had become an accepted ideal for most black men, an ideal that would be reinforced by twentieth-century norms.[5]

The next section illustrates the ways that Black men embody a lack of empathy for the experiences of women.

LACKING EMPATHY AND SUPPORT FOR THE EXPERIENCES AND AMBITIONS OF WOMEN

The men in this book had difficulty naming and exhibiting empathy for the experiences of women. During the interviews, they took an extended amount of time, with seconds of silence in between, before offering responses to the question, *"What does it mean to be a woman?"* This is in stark contrast to their quick and passionate responses to questions on the experiences of Black men. Specifically, Kendrick, Eddie, and Jamal paused between three and seven seconds before offering their perspectives. In response to the question, *"What does it mean to be a woman?,"* Kendrick expressed,

> What it means to be a woman? (three seconds of silence pass). I couldn't tell you, cuz I'm not. So there is no way for me to explain it to you . . . [but] I don't know if it takes more to be a woman. I don't know. That's like if I had a daughter, I would rather my ex-wife to raise her than me trying to raise her because I don't know what it's like to be a woman. And the same retrospect—I would like to be able to be in my son's life more because my ex-wife don't know how to raise him. . . . But yeah as far as what it means to be a woman? I don't know. You have to ask a woman that question.

Similarly, Jamal responded by first repeating the question,

> What does it mean to be a woman? (Seven seconds of silence pass). I don't even think a woman knows what it means to be a woman. Uh (slight laugh). Uh. I don't know. In what aspect? How do you mean? A woman as in a career-driven woman? Or a woman as in just a general I guess outlook on how she's supposed to be towards a man? I don't understand the question.

I clarified the question with Jamal, "the same way you described what it means to be a man, how would you describe what you imagine it means to be a woman?" Jamal responded, "I guess women go through a lot of mixed emotions through a day." Elaborating on what he meant by mixed emotions, Jamal said,

> I just try to stay out the way. Um, I understand women overthink a lot of things and not thinking consciously or realistically about the overthinking that they're doing. So you know in turn they just continue to overthink things. Um, but I guess, seeing as how I'm young, I'm twenty-five, I've run into a lot of women, a lot of girls my age or younger that would always say, "I'm so sad. I feel like I'ma be alone forever." And I would say, "Forever? And we're only nineteen or we're only twenty-two. You really think that if you don't find anyone right now that you'll be alone forever?" And that's just one small aspect about what a woman thinks about throughout her day, which I don't understand how you can feel that way being that young. But like I said: misdirection of thinking. If you were thinking more along the lines of what you wanted to be when you grew up or try to go at what you wanted to be instead of thinking about relationships or what a man can do for you, or what a woman can do for a man, that will come . . . women just do a lot of thinking in a lot of different directions. Me personally, I just think that they go a lot of different ways and they stress themselves out.

Here, we can observe that Jamal accuses women of "not thinking realistically," "overthinking," and embodying "misdirection of thinking." This stance toward women is problematic, at least in part, because it prevents Black men from accurately understanding, naming, and having empathy for the experiences of women.

Let's take a moment to engage Eddie's response to the question, *"What does it mean to be a woman?"* After hearing the question, Eddie initially took a moment to think and then responded, "That's a very dynamic [question]. . . . It's kind of hard as a man to give perspective of what it is to be a woman. I would say it's a struggle." Eddie's response to this and similar questions throughout his interviews indicated that he may be the most aware of all the men in this study regarding the experiences of women. While he also took time (four seconds of silence) to respond to the question, he demonstrated greater awareness and provided a nuanced perspective on the dynamic life of women, including its challenges. Although we can determine that it is a positive attribute for Eddie to embody such an awareness, we can also determine it problematic that just one of the five men in this study maintained a nuanced and empathic stance toward the experiences of women.

The narratives above demonstrate that the men in this book had difficulty identifying the experiences of women and extending empathy for women's experiences in the world. What contributes to this reality? Three observations on the aforementioned narratives will help us explore an answer to this question. First, there is an implicit belief that men are not capable of understanding the experiences of women, and vice versa. As a result of this dimension of patriarchy, the men in this study believe that only a man can raise a man. Likewise, only a woman can raise a woman. What are the implications of this ideology? In my view, it functions as a cop out so that Black men do not have to understand the experiences of women. A similar argument could be made for women understanding the experiences of men. However, this is not the focus of my argument for two reasons. First, history and the perpetuation of patriarchal cultural norms are on the side of men. Consequently, men have unjustly benefited from positions of power so that men can function just fine without having to understand the experiences of women. Second, this book is concerned with improving the mental health of Black men.

I hold that a relational and intersubjective understanding of the world is beneficial and requires an embrace of an attitude which seeks to understand the other. Why is this important? From an intersubjective perspective, we all have an impact on one another. In this light, ignoring female experience prohibits Black men from developing and maintaining an awareness of the mutual impact of human lives. From an intersubjective perspective, Black men should listen and seek to understand the experiences of the other, even those dimensions of human experiences which are not innately familiar to our own experience in the world. As such, it is problematic to maintain a

Black male identity that does not seek to understand the experiences of women. Similarly, it is not adequate to opt out of developing and maintaining an awareness of female experience primarily on the basis that one is not a woman.

Possessing an awareness of female experience includes tending to the emotions of women. Speaking on the emotions of women, Jamal says, "I just try to stay out the way." Is this approach helpful for developing and maintaining empathy for the experiences of women? I suggest that it is not a helpful approach. Rather, what would it look like for Black men to thoughtfully consider and journey with women's—particularly Black women's—emotional experiences? I am not implying that men are the only responsible party in this matter. However, improvising off the words of Jamal, Black men have the responsibility to "stay in the way" with Black women, not in the abusive and life-denying sense, but in a way that faithfully journeys with women to foster possibilities of human flourishing for Black women. Black male flourishing necessarily includes developing and maintaining empathy for the experiences of women. A Hope to Keep Going framework for care and counseling is particularly concerned that Black men have empathy and maintain support for the experiences and ambitions of Black women.

A second observation from the aforementioned narratives recognizes that there is an implicit belief that the lives of women are too difficult to understand, even for women. From this vantage point, the lives of women are deemed by Black men to be fundamentally confusing. This belief is embraced to the extent that Jamal said, "even a woman [doesn't know] what it means to be a woman." Black men in this book possess a belief that womanhood is inherently confusing and not normal. One might say that this second point is similar to the first. True in certain regards. They are related, and yet a distinctive of this second point is that there is an embedded belief that womanhood within itself is too difficult for anyone to understand. From this view, neither men nor women can understand the experiences of women. As Jamal states, "I don't even think a woman knows what it means to be a woman." This view is problematic because it maintains that womanhood is inherently unfamiliar to humans. As a result, female experience is "othered" by men. A manifestation of this form of "othering" is that Black men can live without considering the experiences of women as normative. Consequently, experiences of women are not given the adequate care and attention needed for women to flourish. This is a function of male privilege that must be continually challenged by caregivers working with Black men.

The third observation from the aforementioned narratives recognizes that there is an accusatory tone toward the mental processing of women. This includes the belief that women engage in "misdirection of thinking." An example of this dynamic is blaming women for overthinking. Accusatory and non-empathic attitudes toward women do not allow men to listen and understand why women mentally process and act in particular ways. The inquiry of why women think and act as they do is significant, because it allows men to consider the various cultural, familial, historical, and intrapsychic realities that affect women. From my clinical counseling experience, I'm reminded that there are always reasons why individuals think and act as they do. By maintaining an attitude that seeks to consider why women think and act as they do, Black men can embody empathy rather than embody and exude accusatory attitudes toward women. Theories and practices of care and counseling should nurture in Black men an ability to listen and to seek to understand the experiences of women in order to eliminate the practice of blaming women for overthinking and engaging in "misdirection of thinking."

Ultimately, possessing accusatory and non-empathic attitudes toward the experiences of women is problematic and has far-reaching consequences for communal life. It limits possibilities for life-affirming relationships between women and men because it does not normalize the experiences of women. Anything outside of the experiences of men receives limited attention because it is treated as subservient to the experiences of men. A consequence of this reality is when Black men appreciate women solely for the pleasure that women bring to men. Viewing women solely through this lens is indeed problematic and functions as ammunition to perpetuate abusive and violent relationships men often have with women.

APPRECIATING WOMEN FOR
THE PLEASURE WOMEN BRING TO MEN

An ethical person would certainly agree that women exist for more than the purpose of pleasuring men. Such a person would acknowledge that women exist for a variety of purposes that transcend patriarchal conceptions of womanhood. Yet, society continues to portray women, particularly Black women, as objects for pleasure. Given this cultural reality, it is critical for all men to rid ourselves of unconscious and conscious views of women which are derivatives of patriarchal cultural norms. Men in this book demonstrated that they appreciated women for the pleasure women bring to men. Additionally, they seem to embrace a belief that men cannot exist without women. The approach in this project does not assert that women can never bring pleasure to men. Rather, I am arguing that it is problematic when men view women solely through the lens of a pleasure-seeking ego. Exploring examples of men appreciating women for the pleasure women bring to men will be helpful for our analysis. Matthew declared that women are the "Yin to the Yang of the man. A beautiful creature, one who, a species I particularly appreciate (said with laughter)." Eddie also expressed his appreciation for women:

So it's kinda hard to say being a man what it is to be a woman, but I would say to be a woman is beautiful. I love women. I love black women most in particular. But I love just the shape of women, how they look. Even when touching them, it feels good. But I don't want to take it to the point where I'm touching in a disrespectful manner. So maybe a hug, maybe a handshake. It all depends on what the woman wants.

In addition to Matthew and Eddie, Jamal exhibited appreciation for women. His appreciation was communicated through body language rather than words. While Jamal and I were conducting our second interview, two young Black females walked past us on the sidewalk. As they walked past, Jamal paused from his response to my interview questions to get a view of the young women walking through the neighborhood. Three seconds of silence passed by. Jamal then laughed. His thought process being altered, he attempted to resume our conversation by finishing his response to the interview question. Yet, he laughed again as he continued. While Jamal did not explicitly say anything about the two women who walked by us during the interview, my interpretation is that he was attracted to the two women and momentarily paused our conversation to get a better view of the two women whose very presence he found attractive. Although this is all speculative on my behalf, I imagine it is a well-informed speculation, further demonstrating the ways that some Black men appreciate Black women solely for the pleasure that Black women bring to Black men.[6] Citing a response by Kendrick will help reinforce this point. Responding to the question, *"What does it means to be a woman?"* Kendrick expressed, "I mean from my perspective what I would want in a woman is not a definition of a woman, just be a perspective." What is interesting here is that I did not ask Kendrick his thoughts on what he "would want in a woman." Rather, the question posed to him was, *"What does it mean to be a woman?"* While I was interested in Kendrick's perspective on the experiences of women, he moved to name his desires of what he "would want in a woman." This is another example of men thinking of women primarily from the vantage point of imagining the pleasure that women can bring to men as opposed to allowing the experiences of women to stand on their own, free of the burden of satisfying the needs of men.

I am not suggesting that Black men cannot exhibit appreciation for women. Rather, I am arguing that Black men should appreciate women for more than the pleasure that women can bring to men. It is to suggest that Black men ought to appreciate and acknowledge the whole of a woman's struggles, triumphs, personality, and way of being in the world. This type of life-affirming appreciation for women is made difficult by the existence of at least two dynamics observed in the participant responses above. First, there is the notion that women are the "Yin to the Yang" for men. There are certainly positive aspects to this concept of male-female relationships. However, this can also be problematic when a man feels that he needs a woman and cannot exist without her. It is true that we all need others to exist. This human need is particularly heightened in Black men because of the systemic forces of racism. Yet, the question must be raised whether a woman should be expected to be the primary bearer to meet the complex needs of Black men whom society views as monsters. And, yet, perhaps the more appropriate question for spiritual caregivers, counselors, and community leaders is, *How can we help Black men explore and identify resources within oneself and in the community so that women, particularly Black women, don't bear the heavy burden of meeting all the needs of Black men?* I am not suggesting that Black women and Black men cannot be mutually supportive as both attempt to survive and flourish in a racist society. Rather, I am suggesting that a man's desperation for a woman can lead him to act in violent and abusive ways when he does not get what he wants from a woman. Second, the narratives above indicate that the men in this book appreciate the physical shape and touch of women. Appreciating women primarily for their shape and the feel of their touch is problematic. When this is the norm, Black men perpetuate the legacy of viewing women primarily as objects of pleasure. Such an objectification too often includes viewing women as objects whose sole purpose is to meet the emotional and physical needs of men. Liberative theories and practices of care should work to eradicate Black male identities that objectify women, particularly the lives of Black women.

IDENTIFYING WOMEN AS MOTHERING, LOVING, CARING, AND UNDERSTANDING

One of the ways that men receive pleasure is through being mothered, loved, cared for, and understood by women. The men in this book named these attributes when asked to describe what it means to be a woman. We can deduce that these attributes can function to meet the emotional and physical needs of men.[7] When asked to give his perception of what it means to be a woman, Matthew said,

> Um again, equally as strong as a man. Um, you know, so we don't even have that (laughs) inkling of chauvinist popping this conversation . . . Um, again that more talented helper of the two (said with laughter). Cuz women are the master facilitators and multi-taskers. A woman is a life-giver, a mother. . . . And honestly the whole thing is they're taking care of us (said with laughter), you know. . . . Um, and we all came from mothers. You know we wouldn't be here if it weren't for our mothers. So you know they are nurturers, life-givers, excellent organizers, the stronger of the two sexes, honestly (said with laughter).

Kendrick put it this way, "but for me what I consider to be a woman: just be loving and caring, and understanding." Darrell responded to the question of what it means to be a woman by saying,

> See I feel as if they both got 'man' in there. So, I feel like a woman is a different type of human being. She could also be a provider too. But I feel like her role is more catered to the man, helping out. They work together. But she's also a provider too. Um, she's more like a person that, um, takes care of the family as well.

Our observations here might seem obvious. The men in this book primarily view women as caretakers of men and families. As Chanequa Walker-Barnes articulates, there is a tremendous burden of strength placed on women, Black women in particular, when women are expected to live for the purpose of taking care of the needs of others. One of my reactions while engaging men's responses in this chapter was, "well who's taking care of Black women?" This question is not originally posed in this study, but was previously raised by womanist scholars concerned with the well-being of Black women. This project, too, concerned with the well-being of women, argues that Black men must be concerned to help nurture the flourishing of women, so that Black male flourishing necessarily includes a thoughtful, caring, and empathic concern for women.

There have been Black men who attempted—and continue to attempt—to transcend patriarchal notions of Black masculinity. bell hooks writes that,

> Despite the overwhelming support of patriarchal masculinity by black men, there was even in slavery those rare black males who repudiated the norms set by white oppressors. . . . In southern states enclaves of African folk who had escaped slavery or joined with renegade maroons once slavery ended kept alive African cultural retentions that also offered a subculture distinct from the culture imposed by whiteness. [8]

It is, therefore, important for Black men—and those caring for Black men—to acknowledge, develop, and continue to imagine and re-imagine Black masculinity in manners that are distinct from oppressive White patriarchal norms of masculinity.

CONCLUSION

I have explored four subthemes which name the ways that Black men in this book understand themselves in relation to women: *1) Identifying men as providers and protectors*; *2) Lacking empathy for the experiences of women*; *3) Appreciating women for the pleasure women bring to men*; and *4) Identifying women as motherly, loving, caring, and understanding.* While all four can be critiqued for strands of patriarchal ideology embedded within them, the first three subthemes must be critiqued for their power to perpetuate hegemonic norms of Black male identity, which are in opposition to the flourishing of women. The tendency of Black men to embody a masculine identity characterized by the primary roles of provider and protector without developing and maintaining empathy and support for the experiences and ambitions of women is problematic. Negative images, expectations, and treatment of Black men in society have driven Black men to act aggressively toward women. At this juncture it is important to make explicit the position held here that it is never acceptable for Black men to take feelings of aggression out on the lives of women. Rather, other life-giving coping mechanisms must be identified, adopted, and developed in the lives of Black men. Ultimately, this chapter argues that caring for the mental health of Black men includes fostering safe spaces for Black men to imagine and re-imagine Black male identities which will promote not only the flourishing of Black men, but also the flourishing of Black women. Human flourishing for Black men, then, necessarily includes developing and maintaining empathy and support for the experiences and ambitions of Black women so that men and women will flourish together in community.

NOTES

1. bell hooks, *We Real Cool,* 138.
2. hooks, *We Real Cool,* xvi.
3. hooks, *We Real Cool,* 141.
4. Here I am concerned with professional, platonic, and romantic relationships with women.
5. hooks, *We Real Cool,* 4.
6. In this case, there appears to be a heterosexual attraction on behalf of Jamal toward the two Black women walking past us on the sidewalk. I am not intending to make heterosexuality the norm. In the case of this study, however, the Black men appear to embody heterosexual attractions toward women.
7. Here, I am inferring that a man's physical needs can be met by women, namely in the case of heterosexual relationships.
8. hooks, *We Real Cool,* 4.

Chapter Four

Intertwined Worlds in the Mind

What occurs in the minds of Black men? The interviews in this study revealed that the psyches of Black men carry the added burden of having to wrestle with negative cultural images and expectations of themselves in the media and society. That is, Black men cannot escape being treated as subservient objects in society, who are disrespected, disregarded, discredited, feared, and devalued throughout their lives. Treated in this way presents dangers to the mental health of Black men. Specifically, the psyches of Black men are at greater risk of being wounded due to cultural environments that are not conducive to the flourishing of Black male psyches. While chapter three addressed sexist dimensions of Black male identity, this chapter focuses on the impact of racism on intersubjective reality in the psyches of Black men. In this chapter, I am concerned with addressing the following question: How do the psyches of Black men deal with realities of being surrounded by social contexts which perpetuate negative images and expectations of Black men? While money and enhanced social standing may enable a Black man to dodge a few bullets (metaphorically and literally) from a racist culture, even the wealthiest and most well-respected Black man faces moments when his life cannot escape the negative cultural blows to his psyche. Pledging allegiance to the category of race and the workings of racism, the media and society treat Black men as "less-than" objects of history who must remain subservient in the social order. The claim here is that dominant American and global cultures, which remain committed to the category of race and the workings of racism, cause psychological harm to the mental health of Black men. Negative cultural images and expectations of Black men, perpetuated by the media and society, function as barriers to the flourishing of Black men.

Living amidst oppressive cultures that pose threats to the mental health of Black men, the men in this book demonstrate that their minds are active. With active minds, they seek to understand and process their experiences while wrestling with the negative images and expectations culture holds for them as Black men. Their lives demonstrate that negative cultural images and expectations of Black men are in opposition to the ideals and visions they have for their own lives. In this sense, they maintain visions for their lives which transcend racist images and expectations that American and global cultures have for Black men. The fact that their minds are actively reflecting on their experiences in the world, and that they have the ability to connect deeply with their emotions, dispels myths that Black men are emotionless beings without psychic capacity to reflect deeply and critically. The men in this book demonstrated that their psychological lives are complex. In this sense, the psychological lives of Black men should not be assessed solely through the rubrics of psychological theories which were constructed by and for White people. Rather, in order to achieve human flourishing, the psychological tasks of Black men include: 1) understanding the nuances of how one is related to in a racist world; and 2) determining how best to participate in it. This reality makes the psychological life of Black men unique and distinct from, for instance, White people from whom many psychological and clinical theories are grounded and developed. Society and caregivers, who practice therapy primarily out of White normative models of care, have remained unaware of the psychological activity occurring in the psyches of Black men. The voices of Black men in this book serve as a resource to help us understand better the intrapsychic experiences of Black men.

By engaging the lives of men in this book in their own words, we can observe that Black men have feelings like other human beings. Nonetheless, in the same breath, we can identify categories of psychological life distinct and unique to Black male life. I do not aim to totalize all Black male experience, for difference exists among Black men. Yet, culture's commitment to the category of race and the workings of racism necessarily means that all Black men are negatively affected by racist underpinnings of culture, which continues to attack the psyches of Black men with unrelenting force. This force significantly affects the psychological activity occurring in the minds of Black men. While Black men may not openly talk about nor be fully conscious of the impacts of negative cultural forces in their lives, these forces affect Black men's psychic activity.

Chapters 1 and 3 explored racism's and sexism's impact on the psychological life of Black men. This chapter explicitly considers the intersubjective activity occurring in their psyches, particularly as it relates to racism's impact on psychological life. I want to highlight two critical dimensions of intrapsychic experience in the lives of Black men in this book: *1) An Active Mind*; and *2) Yearning to be Understood*. The first dynamic requires a briefer observation than the second. First, the psyches of the men in this book are extremely active. It is as if an intense internal war occurs in their psyches. Although this mental war significantly affects their day-to-day realities, to them it seems, as explicitly stated by Darrell, that "nobody cares." Yet, caregivers, clinicians, and community leaders have the opportunity to respond to the psychological realities of Darrell and other Black men with an affirmative, "yes, we care." What would the care of Black men look like if the larger community affirmed and cared for the psychological realities of Black men? Second, amidst a cultural climate in which Black men feel as if "nobody cares," the men in this book demonstrated that they yearn to be understood. I observed a definite passion in the voices of the men in this book as they described their life experiences and perspectives. My observation was that they desired to be heard and understood, and were eager to share their life experiences once they determined I was a safe person with whom to share and open up about their life experiences and emotional lives. Throughout our conversations, there were moments when the men followed up their remarks by asking the rhetorical, "you feel me?" Could it be that too often Black men do not feel understood by people in their daily lives? If so, perhaps a result is that Black men have developed the saying, "you feel me?" Exploring the importance of being "felt" or understood, the present chapter is concerned with "feeling" the intersubjective psychological activity occurring in the lives of the Black men. Reflecting on culture and engaging the narratives of the men in this book have led me to make the following observation: emotionally, Black men "can't breathe"[1] in toxic cultural environments in the United States that often and effectively choke the psychological imaginations of Black men. In this sense, it cannot be overstated that the psychological lives of Black men are significantly affected by culture. With the election of President Donald Trump, we have seen a rise in hate crimes and cultural norms that relate to Black and Brown people, Muslims, and other systematically marginalized groups with racist, xenophobic, hegemonic, and imperialist sentiments. White supremacists and the unconsciously racist alike have flocked to Donald Trump in droves[2] as their presidential candidate of choice. Time will tell of the impact of Donald Trump's presidency on the lives of Black people. For the present, I am concerned with gaining in-depth understandings of the psychological life of Black men as affected by cultural norms.

An aim of this chapter is to unpack the intrapsychic activity occurring in the psyches of Black men, which is necessarily affected by culture's negative views and expectations of Black men. A reflection on the following question will aid our exploration: How do the negative cultural blows to the psyches of Black men, from the media and society, affect psychological activity occurring in the psyches of Black men?

Four subthemes on this topic emerged from the interviews with the men in this book and are presented in the following pages to help us respond to the aforementioned question. The subthemes are: *1) Internal Emotions: Hurt, Wounded, Sad, Frustrated, and Angered*; *2) Exerting Energy Imagining the Mindsets of White People*; *3) Resisting*; and *4) Acknowledging Obama, Entertainers, and Social Activists.* The data also pointed to ways in which the men in this book have been affected by early life caregivers and other persons in their lives who had a significant impact in their most formative years. In addition to the four subthemes outlined above, the following subtheme also emerged: *Significant Impact of Early Life Caregivers and Parental Figures.* The men demonstrated that their mothers, fathers, uncles, and grandmothers had a significant impact on their lives. Because there is adequate literature written on this topic, I limit our discussion to the four previously named subthemes in this chapter. Nonetheless, it is important to affirm that a child's early life experiences with caregivers and parental figures have a significant impact on the child's adolescent, young adult, and adult life. As such, parental figures and caretakers should seek to develop empathic attunement with the lives of young Black men.

INTERNAL EMOTIONS: HURT, WOUNDED, SAD, FRUSTRATED, AND ANGERED

bell hooks offers reflections on social factors which often prevent Black men from living healthy emotional lives. She states,

> Whether in an actual prison or not, practically every black male in the United States has been forced at some point in his life to hold back the self he wants to express, to repress and contain fear of being attacked, slaughtered, destroyed. Black males often exist in a prison of the mind unable to find their way out. In patriarchal culture, all males learn a role that restricts and confines. When race and class enter the picture, along with patriarchy, then black males endure the worst impositions of gendered masculine patriarchal identity.[3]

Further, "No one really wants to hear black men speak their pain or offer them avenues of healing."[4] Contrary to these cultural norms, a Hope to Keep Going framework for care and counseling invites Black men to be in touch with their emotions and to, subsequently, consider how engagement with their emotions can inform how they might live creatively and constructively into the future.

As conversations with Black men in this book unfolded, feelings of hurt, woundedness, and sadness, along with the accompanying emotions of frustration and anger emerged. The feelings of frustration and anger seemed to emerge as a response to their chronic feelings of being emotionally hurt, wounded, and sad, which are precipitated by social injustices negatively affecting their intrapsychic experiences. We can surmise that Black men's feelings of frustration and anger are more easily identifiable to the casual observer than feelings of hurt, woundedness, and sadness. However, as psychodynamic theory asserts, there is more than that which what meets the eye. Feelings of sadness in Black men often derive from chronic experiences of being emotionally hurt and wounded in society. Feelings of chronic sadness, hurt, and woundedness have led Black men to feel frustrated and angry. Perhaps underneath Black men's feelings of frustration and anger is the feeling that "I should not be treated like this by the world. It's sad that it keeps happening in my life and I'm frustrated and mad as hell because of it." The claim here is that the emotional lives of Black men are scarred by negative cultural images and expectations of Black men in the media and society. As a result, the feelings of frustration and anger in Black men are responses to the systemic ills of American and global cultures which maintain commitments to the category of race and the workings of racism by which the psychological lives of Black men continue to remain under continual attack.

Earlier, I cited Kendrick's way of dealing with the negative images of Black men in the media and society for which he stated, "I just prove 'em wrong. . . . There's no other way." He further expressed,

> I mean, I see it in the news and it's nothing I can do. But I mean I get frustrated, but you can only get frustrated for so long. Just be myself and not fall victim to their rules and stuff. . . . Like now if somebody calls me a black . . . or a white person may say "nigga" to piss me off, I don't react. I don't give them that reaction because that's what they want. So, I don't do it.

Kendrick acknowledges his frustration concerning the ways Black men are treated by the news media and society. Yet, he also implies that there also come moments when "you can only get frustrated for so long." What happens when Black men no longer have the energy to be frustrated? For now, I assert that nihilism can emerge among Black men, especially after they have been frustrated for long periods of time and believe no relief is in sight. Caring for the mental health of Black men should include a focus on relieving the burdens of systemic racism placed on Black men, while also helping Black men cope with the inevitable frustrations and anger that accompany living life in a society that, systemically, culturally, and institutionally, makes it difficult for Black men to survive and flourish.

Darrell further drives home the point of what it feels like to be a Black man: "It's like playing Monopoly. Everybody starts negative and you only got one dice. White folks got two dice. They going quicker on the board. We only got one dice and the highest number is three." I then asked Darrell, *"What impact does it have on you?"* He responded,

> Um, anger sometimes. Just living this life, I can't. . . . Man how can I say it? Like just seeing my mom. It was tough. She came home one day crying because. . . . I remember one time everybody got a promotion in the room except for her. And she had to just sit there and look at everybody like, "Oh y'all got promotions. More money, and I do the same thing y'all do, but no promotion for me? What's going on? And I've been working here for how many years?" So it's like seeing that and hearing about that just makes me kinda angry. Like, this is how people are treated in corporate America? And I'm going to school to work in that? I can't. That's just not something I wanna do. . . . Also, it makes me kinda sad. Just because my son or daughter is gonna be black and they gonna have to go through the same thing I went through. So it's tough. But it makes you more tough too.

Later, responding to the question, *"What do you do when you feel devalued?,"* Darrell stated, "Like if I feel devalued I just be like, 'dang.' I just stick on it, and never even get out of it." Referring to a situation where he felt devalued and excluded from the group in school, he noted, "Like that situation, I didn't surpass it . . . and I just probably did the 'C' work. You know what I mean? And I just was like it is what it is." Elaborating on what he meant by not getting out of it, Darrell said, "I didn't get out of it. I just stayed in that type of mindset and never got out of it. I got grades back and it was 'C' work I did. My mind was stuck on this is probably what it is. I am that. I'm not a valuable asset. Yeah, I didn't get out of that. That's a lot of situations too." The weight of systemic oppression is severe in Darrell's life. We can observe that he is deeply affected by the ways he and his mother have been unfairly treated by society. He explicitly reflected on how seeing and hearing the ways that his mother (a Black woman) was unfairly treated—namely being passed over after years of service on her job—angered him. In addition, Darrell told me that he gets sad thinking about how his son or daughter will have to go through "the same thing" that he and his mother have gone through as people disadvantaged and treated unfairly in society. Finally, we can observe that he has internalized the thought that he is "not a valuable asset." That there are severe consequences on the psychological lives of Black men—as a result of internalizing the belief that we are "not a valuable asset"—should be clear.

Eddie is perhaps very aware of the ways in which American culture treats Black men as if we're "not a valuable asset." Discussing how he deals with the images of Black men in the media and society, he said,

> I try to speak up on these issues, but it's become a time where a lot of times I feel like I'm a scapegoat cuz I don't agree with the way the media portrays certain things. Like I get attacked by other people in society . . . when people

get upset and attack me, that causes me to become emotional, not by crying tears, but emotions with my anger. Like I might say something that might burn a bridge or destroy a relationship based off of us disagreeing when it shouldn't have to be that way. You can say what you gon' say. I'm not gonna agree with you. You not gonna agree with me. We're not gonna agree on everything, but we can agree to disagree. It's like at a point where people don't want to hear what I have to say. They try to block out what I have to say. So it's frustrating but I have to do it.

Here we can gather that Eddie's feelings of anger derive from being scapegoated after speaking his truth and, ultimately, not being understood.

Jamal also expressed feelings of anger. I asked him what he does when feeling devalued; he responded: "Uh, I contemplate. Sometimes I think maybe, like I said, maybe I should be this way. Um, sometimes it gets me angry and, like I said, as being from where I'm from fighting is always a first instinct for me. Um, I may feel that way sometimes but the, like I said, I just think about real life. I think about consequences." What is important for us here is to observe the mental processing Jamal engages as a response to feeling devalued. We can track his responses in the following sequence: 1) Thinking about giving into the negative expectations that the world has for him as a Black man (this is similar to Darrell's account above); 2) Becoming angry; 3) Possessing the instinct to fight; and 4) Thinking "about real life" and the "consequences" for his actions.

As a final note on the internal emotions of the men in this book, Matthew was the only one not to explicitly name his internal emotions. He appeared to embody a protective coping mechanism, which guards against any psychological vulnerability and prevents him from lamenting. However, I get the sense that there are moments in his life when he does not feel peace. While explaining what he does when feeling devalued, he expressed, "So if it's something I feel like really kind of confused around or trying to understand like, 'what was that all about?' I get on a bike and ride. I do miles. And by the end of that cycle, I normally have an answer or perspective to that question that I posed. It gives me peace and the whole time I'm breathing in and out I'm exercising my soul as well." His response demonstrates that he yearns for peace and, by getting on his bike to ride for miles, he can attain peace in moments of his life when peace is absent. We can surmise that before the bike ride, peace is absent. I imagine that peace is absent for a majority of Black men in this book because of the burden of systemic oppression in their lives. As a metaphor, we might consider: what are the "bike rides" that give Black men peace amidst a hostile cultural environment intent on, effectively, devaluing their lives? I am not interested in a Kumbaya moment in which the social injustices negatively impacting the lives of Black men are ignored. Rather, I am interested in caregivers, clinicians, and community leaders understanding deeply the complexities of Black male psyches which make it difficult for Black men to maintain peace. Peace, in this sense, should be facilitated in Black men even as we work to dismantle racism's negative impact on the psyches of Black men. Likewise, the facilitation of peace in Black men must occur in ways that also promote the flourishing of women, and Black women in particular.

EXERTING ENERGY IMAGINING
THE MINDSETS OF WHITE PEOPLE

Elements of surprise often emerge during qualitative inquiry. The subtheme, *Exerting Energy Imagining the Mindsets of White People,* is perhaps the one that struck me as most astonishing. The men in this book demonstrated that they are aware of the ways, from their vantage point, that they are "looked at" by others in society, particularly through the eyes of White people. This is significant in that it adds an additional stressor to the mental health of Black men. This section explores the impact of being "looked at"—by White people—on the intrapsychic realities of the Black men.

Thinking about White People

Expressing his view on what U.S. society thinks about Black men, Darrell shared,

> I feel like the U.S. society loves the black man. I feel like they love it. But they don't want to admit it. Behind closed doors, white folks are so mad that we doing this or we did this. They just can't stand it when we just doing stuff. I feel like because, it's more like they know we started. . . . They just know we come from a certain cloth. And I feel like they didn't come from that. They just steal. They do whatever they need to get where they at.

According to Darrell, White people like Black men yet neither acknowledge the accomplishments of Black men nor want to see Black men succeed. Further, he believes White people steal from Black people "to get where they at." Such a view means that Black men are likely to embody a disposition in which Black men don't trust White people because of a fear that White people will steal from Black men to fulfill White people's own needs and desires. While all White people are not the same, it is hard to argue against this stance. History verifies that White people have stolen from the lives and accomplishments of Black people. This is evident in the arts where White executives have taken the talent of Black people in music, particularly jazz and hip hop, and other art forms, for economic gain, only to leave Black people with a smaller chunk of the pie. This can also be seen in sports where African American athletes' salaries are pale compared to the revenue of wealthy White owners of sports franchises. While this dynamic is evident in sports and music, it is not limited to these realms and can be observed in other areas of professional and personal life in which Black people provide the talent and White people reap significant economic and personal gain. The point here is that Black men, like Darrell, are cognizant of this reality and must negotiate, as such, relationships with White people, fully aware of this potential danger. In this sense, a dimension of the mental health of Black men consists of knowing how to protect ourselves from having our own ideas and talents stolen by White people for their own economic and personal gain. This has been and continues to be a detriment to the economic and personal lives of Black men.

Not only do the men in this book exert energy thinking how White people possess the ability to steal from the idea, and talents of Black men, they also exert energy thinking of how White people fear their very existence. Describing how he is seen by White people, Jamal stated,

> What they see is what they see in movies or what they see in TV . . . a guy that will snatch your purse and more likely will snatch your purse or snatch your iPhone or take something from you that you worked hard for. That's pretty much all they see in me. Um, you know. Even though I dress nice; even though, like I said, I may have a pocket full of money on me, but that doesn't matter to them because that's not what they see, you know. And I just, you know . . . I guess in some ways it gets me angry and some ways I feel that I should do what they expect of me, but in some ways that's not doing any good at all. . . . I think that if you're intelligent and you can show them that you're intelligent, that's what really truly angers them, angers others. So yeah. I would say I try to do that. I try to understand more about life and their way of getting over, you know, so that I can respectfully and cordially smile and get over, I guess, you know. Help a way for us to be better.

We can observe that Jamal is aware that "dressing nice" and having "a pocket full of money" means nothing to White people, because they already see him a certain way and have expectations of him. These expectations, as someone deemed a threat, angers Jamal, yet are so powerful that in moments he finds himself wanting to give into these very expectations. According to Jamal, the way to counter White people's perception and treatment of him is to: 1) be intelligent; 2) understand "their way of getting over;" and 3) respectfully and cordially smile when in the presence of White people.

Acknowledging the Power of White People

Discussing how he deals with negative images of Black men in the media, Darrell shared,

Like I said before, I don't watch too much of the tube. But I just try to educate myself more. I prepare myself so I won't be that black man. I know that I easily can, cuz they [White people] can fire me quick. But I just try to prepare myself and educate myself to be better than what I was before, or yesterday so I can continue to be a better person, and just keep positivity around my circle; like listening to motivational speakers . . . I know they be like, "Man he black. I know he just hate being around us." But I just try to stay positive and be happy around all that. I just try to stay positive. That's just how I deal with everything. I just try to stay positive.

Accepting that White people have more power than Blacks, and specifically to "fire me quick," Darrell's approach is to prepare and educate himself while remaining positive amidst the circumstances. Given the contextual reality of Black people in America, we can conjecture that a necessary dimension of psychological life for Black men is to possess the mindset always to educate and prepare ourselves.

Comparing Black Experience to White Experience

Reflecting on the question, *"What does it mean when a person is treated as if he's invisible?,"* Kendrick stated,

I guess like, you're not being noticed. . . . Say I went into Tiffany's dressed bummy and I'm black. They'll probably be like, "naw, I ain't gonna bother him." But if a white guy dressed up went in there, they may approach him like, "Hey, can we help you?" And I've been in situations where I went to a restaurant, sat there, and nobody said nothing. Then three or four people came in, [and the restaurant workers were like], "oh yeah, here, here." I left. (Kendrick laughs) I'm like ok. . . . That's not even cool. It's just like, they don't even expect. That's like we walk into a Bentley dealership. If they don't know me, then they not gonna pay no attention to me. It's that type of invisibility I don't like.

Additionally, Kendrick reflected on how he and a Puerto Rican colleague were treated on their job compared to how he imagined a White person would be treated in the same scenario. While the following quote was referenced in chapter 1, I present it again here to help us reflect on the manner in which Kendrick compares the Black experience to the White experience:

Perfect example! I was working for AT&T. . . . If I was a white guy with all this stuff on walking in people's yard, they would not have said nothing. They called the police on me and this Puerto Rican guy. We got the [company] helmet, jacket, vest, everything on. And they like, "What y'all doing?" [Kendrick responded]: "Working! Why you talking about 'what are we doing?'" So it's invisibility sometimes when they don't want to be bothered with you and then other times it's very noticeable and arrogant.

Kendrick is highlighting a reality in the psyches of Black men that they are treated differently than White people and are not allotted the same privileges granted White people, such as being accepted and deemed credible.

Jamal also compared the treatment of Blacks and Whites:

> Something that just recently happened with the thing in Charleston with the white boy. Excuse me, with the Caucasian male (slight laughter). That gentleman you know killed nine people and was able to get a private flight. He got him a vest. . . . He even got a cheeseburger, you know, on the way to jail or whatever he is right now at this moment where he is supposed to be anyway. He's just troubled. He's twenty, he's a grown man. And I had recently just saw a young [black] kid get almost basically life in jail for killing a police dog, you know, or something of that nature. He got no bail. He got nothing of that nature and it was an animal. I understand whatever the case may be, but just a lot of days, a lot of times we are being portrayed as evil people when we're not."

In Jamal's mind, Black men are treated as if we're evil people. Yet, White people are allotted luxuries, such as a private jet and a cheeseburger, even when having committed a crime. In other words, when White people engage in criminal activity, they are not treated as criminals. Yet, even when Black people exert energy thinking about the power and mindsets of Whites and try to abide by their rules, we are still thought to be threats and are treated as criminals.

PSYCHOLOGICAL RESISTANCE

Psychological resistance can function as a powerful tool for making possible opportunities to survive and flourish amidst cultural environments saturated with White supremacist ideology. I have inserted the word "opportunities" before the words "survive" and "flourish" because I do not want to communicate a false impression that as long as a Black man resists oppression, all the worries of the world will go away. This is not true. In fact, becoming aware of the evils of the world may initially (and even continually) trouble one's soul with intense emotions. However, by facing the truth of our existence, we can effectively resist forces of oppression in such a way that makes possible our survival, liberation, healing, and flourishing. Black men give ourselves a fighting chance to survive, live a meaningful life, and ultimately flourish when we are aware of the systemic and cultural trappings of racism, and all forms of oppression, and work to resist them with every fiber in our being. Hence, this section explores the ways that the men in this book psychologically resist amidst the negative cultural images and expectations of themselves in the media and society.[5] I highlight psychological resistance in their lives by naming the ways that they: 1) turn away from negativity; 2) "prove them wrong" while redefining negative narratives of Black men; and 3) refuse subservient status.

Turning Away from Negativity

One of the ways that Matthew and Darrell resist the negative images and expectations of Black men is simply by turning away from the negativity about Black men present in the media and society. The example of Darrell is helpful for unpacking this reality: "I don't watch TV. It's too much negativity on the black man. Like the shootings with the police. [They say] it's not about race. [But] it's always about race. It's somebody died. A human died. It's too racist. So I try to get that negativity out of my head. I don't want to watch it." He later explained, "I just try to stay positive. That's just how I deal with everything. I just try to stay positive. I try not to blame people because I'm black. I know that's the case, but I try not to do it the majority of the time. I try not to do that. I just try to stay positive." Darrell later said,

> So, I try to keep myself out of the black and white thing just because it's tough on the mind. You know going through life being black is already tough, so I just try to stay positive. Another thing I do is. . . . I'm trying to be an entrepreneur. I want to be an entrepreneur and I keep my mind busy on that versus listening to TV and being informed about why . . . just always being informed about black men, I don't want to be on that. So, I'm meeting with another guy after this just to keep my head glued on entrepreneurial shit. Just trying to keep myself focused.

In this case, Darrell avoids negativity about Black men and chooses to stay positive. One of the ways he stays positive is to pursue and remain focused on entrepreneurial endeavors. We can surmise that the mental activity at play here is the pursuit of an alternative reality, which counters the negative images and expectations of Black men in the media and society. Yet, not only must Darrell pursue such an alternative reality, he must remain focused on it.

He later explained why it's important for him to embrace positive thinking in this season of his life:

> I used to think anything that happened wrong was because I was black. Like I didn't get a job because I was black. I never thought positive. So when you just self-inflicting yourself on those words, it's kinda . . . perception is reality. And what you say is reality, and it comes to life. So then you start thinking like that and then trying to just be like, "I can't get a job, because I'm black." So then you don't want to get a job. You not motivated cuz you know if you apply you're not going to get the job because you're black. So then it's like that is just a downward spiral. And then your relationships are suffering too because now you're in that space where you're just negative.

Most immediately, we can declare that it is important for theories of care and counseling to intervene in such a way that Black men do not fall victim to the downward spiral that Darrell has named. To avoid the downward spiral, Darrell embraced the belief that affirms that if one thinks positively, one will achieve a positive outcome. His positive thinking includes pursuing and remaining focused on alternative realities that counter those in culture which display Black men in negative lights. Listening deeply to Darrell's narrative, we can observe two dimensions of a Black man's life that he believes are negatively affected when a Black man thinks negatively about his identity and life options: 1) *his outlook on life*; and 2) *his relationships.* Perhaps Darrell's belief hints at a reality that without an ability to handle the negative images and expectations of oneself as a Black man, one is in prime position to embody a negative outlook on life which leads to a downward spiral. Similarly, the inability to handle negative images and expectations of ourselves negatively affects Black men's platonic and romantic relationships.

Proving Them Wrong and Redefining Cultural Narratives of Black Men

Earlier, we observed that the men in this book aimed to prove wrong the negative cultural images and expectations that society has of Black men. In this section, I bring attention to the mental activity occurring in the psyches of Black men correlated to their expressed need to prove wrong culture's negative images and expectations of Black men. Kendrick provided a concrete example of this approach when expressing, "I just prove 'em wrong." During our interview, he told me that he enjoys proving wrong the negative expectations that White people have of him. Kendrick is not alone in embodying this approach. The other men in this book also embody mindsets that seek to prove wrong the negative images and expectations American and global cultures have of them as Black men. Responding to the question, *"What does it mean to be a Black man today?,"* Kendrick said, "You just gotta learn how to control yourself and don't give people that stereotype. That's what I try to avoid. When they see you they like, 'oh he's black.' But I have a bachelor's degree and I'm not your typical black guy that you think that you see on TV."

Additionally, Kendrick embodied the belief that a Black man must think strategically, as opposed to reacting before thinking, while interacting with White people. He expressed, "Yeah, you gotta think. You have to. You have to always think before you react. If you react first then think about it later, you gonna come up with several different scenarios you could have did differently if you would have thought it out first." This is an important dimension of human flourishing for Black men; namely, Black men must possess the capacity to think things through first, in the midst of frustration, rage, hurt, and anger, before reacting. We can categorize this as the capacity for self-regulation in the midst of oppressive cultural images, expectations, and treatment. To flourish, Black men must possess an awareness of the potential dangers we face interacting with White people before reacting. Such an awareness functions as a resource while Black men are thinking before reacting.

Matthew also engages a process of thinking before reacting. Describing how he deals with negative images of Black men in the media and society, Matthew expressed that,

> I treat it like a doctor treating an illness. I approach it in the same way. I am a healer. I'm a spiritual healer. So I say, "ok, what is this imagery doing to the mindset?" Alright, so what do we have to do to create an antidote for that mindset? What do we have to talk about? What do we have to create in real world activity? And how do we do that and what does it look like?

In this sense, Matthew engages in a thorough process of thinking before he reacts. He further stated,

> And so I create a curriculum around it. And I go in on it. As opposed to lamenting about it and woe is me-ing, and I know it's plenty of corners in this city that I could roll up on and jump right into the, "man that's messed up conversation." But that's not my life . . . That's how I deal with it. I create solutions. . . . So it's about redefining the rites of passages. We know the ignorance they're spewing. The ignorance is always going to be there. It's about being the light in the midst of that darkness.

After thinking, he develops what he believes is the solution to the "illness" of negative cultural images and expectations of Black men. While we can observe that the men in this book value thinking before reacting, we have not yet identified how Black men should think before reacting. Black men need resources to help them constructively and creatively reflect upon the situations they face before reacting to them. That is, for Black men to flourish, it is not enough to simply think before reacting. Rather, Black men must reflect constructively and creatively before reacting to achieve life-giving results in their lives and in the lives of others.

Another example displaying how a man in this book deals with the negative images and expectations of Black men in the cultural milieu will be helpful. Jamal described his process for countering negative images and expectations of Black men in the media and society in this way:

> What they[6] see is what they see in movies or what they see in TV . . . a guy that will snatch your purse and more likely will snatch your purse or snatch your iPhone or take something from you that you worked hard for. That's pretty much all they see in me. . . . I guess in some ways it gets me angry and

some ways I feel that I should do what they expect of me, but in some ways that's not doing any good at all. All I would be doing is proving to them, you know, that they're right and what they see in TV is right and things like that. So I try not to do those things. I try not to be angry and just try to be as nice and cordial as possible just to I guess be that little dot in the crazy place, you know. Be the little right; the positive dot, you know; the little spec on earth that could possibly change everything else really. That's all. Maybe one day I'll be able to do it in a broader sense.

Here we can observe that Jamal senses that society fears him as a Black man and to counter this fear and the negative expectations society has of him, he tries not to be angry but rather cordial and nice. He stated that people in society only see him as a threat who possesses the real danger of stealing their possessions they have worked so hard to obtain. This is significant when we consider the reality that society, and particularly White-dominated society, seeks to eliminate those things which they fear. In this sense, Black men like Jamal are not to be respected and accepted as human beings, but should be related to as objects to be discarded.

The men in this book display a belief that they, as Black men, must work hard to counter and prove wrong the negative images and expectations society has of Black men so that they will not be discarded but, rather, have an opportunity to survive and flourish in American and global contexts. For our reflections, we should consider: *What are the psychological effects of always having to work harder, to give 110 percent as some might say, as a Black man?* Are Black men built to give 110 percent all the time? While some Black men have learned effective ways to live in a racist society, caring for the mental health of Black men necessarily entails tending to the emotional consequences of having to always be "on" in order to prove wrong the negative images and expectations of themselves as Black men in society. Black men must have safe spaces to let down their guards and be human in order to experience moments of rest and peace amidst oppressive social environments. However, even when Black men have safe spaces to let down their guards, safe spaces should not embody sexist and homophobic ideology. In practice, this is done by respecting Black men while simultaneously pushing Black men to imagine and re-imagine Black masculinities free from domineering attitudes towards women and members of the LGBTQIA community.

Refusing Subservient Status

American and global cultures project onto Black men an ideal that we are subservient objects in the social order. That is, projection has such a tremendous impact on the psyches of people—and for our purposes those of Black men—that it is difficult to resist, in large part, because it is an unconscious activity. In addition, it does not allow the object of projection to exist outside of the qualities and attitudes projected onto the object. Projection, therefore, distorts the identity of the object. The identities of Black men have been distorted in the media and society because of cultures' projections onto the lives of Black men. As Nancy McWilliams notes,

> In its malignant forms, projection breeds dangerous misunderstanding and untold interpersonal damage. When the projected attitudes seriously distort the object on whom they are projected, or when what is projected consists of disowned and highly negative parts of the self, all kinds of difficulties can ensue. Others resent being misperceived and may retaliate. . . . A person who uses projection as his or her main way of understanding the world and coping with life, and who denies or disavows what is being projected, can be said to have a paranoid character.[7]

In this sense, we can assert that White-dominated culture projects unwanted parts of itself onto the lives of Black men as a way to cope with life. Viewed through the lens of McWilliams' description of the paranoid character as articulated above, we can assert that White-dominated culture is in fact paranoid, and by disavowing those parts of itself which are not acceptable to White people, projects those parts of itself onto Black men. Consequently, White-dominated culture, and all those abiding by its ideology,[8] finds a way effectively to cope with life by projecting onto Black men its own feelings and traits, which it must disavow. This has been the case throughout American history and continues, in visible ways, with cases of police brutality against unarmed Black men.

We can further grasp the significance of projection on the psyches of Black men when considering the accompanying process of introjection. McWilliams observes, "Introjection is the process whereby what is outside is misunderstood as coming from inside. . . . In its problematic forms, introjection can, like projection, be highly destructive."[9] Black men are susceptible to introjecting the negative images and expectations of themselves present in the media and society. Additionally, and causing further harm to the psyches of Black men, not only do American and global cultures *unconsciously* relate to Black men in these ways, but also many individuals in American society exhibit very *conscious* and blatant racist treatment toward Black men. Such treatment is oppressive to the psyches of Black men. The combination of unconscious projections and consciously blatant racist acts toward Black men means that in order to survive, and have opportunities to flourish, Black men must possess the psychological ability to resist the forces of projection and the accompanying process of introjection in which Black men identify with the negative images and expectations of themselves which derive from a culture committed to the category of race and the workings of racism. Yet, against these deeply penetrating forces of projection onto Black male psyches, the men in this study demonstrated that they refuse to exist as subservient objects in the social order. The following narratives highlight the ways that they resist negative images and expectations of Black men.

When I asked Matthew to describe a time in his life when he felt devalued, he stated,

> Wouldn't allow it to happen. Internally I would be able to look and see, "oh they're just weaker individuals. They just don't understand." So I would never take it on as a personal definition. So that's a real challenging question for me honestly. Really, I try to think of it, but I just can't. It's just something innate in me that's caused me to always feel like I'm supposed to be here and I'm doing everything regardless of what you all don't understand. It will never affect me.

How does Matthew possess this ability to re-frame the situation so that it does not negatively affect him? Perhaps the answer is found in the presence of his grandmother, extended family, and spirituality, which enables him to resist the negative cultural images and expectations projected onto Black men. These resources in his life enable him to maintain his identity and purpose that counters and transcends the negative cultural images and expectations of Black men. His approach allows him to fend off dangers to his psyche so that he can still function. Yet, perhaps there is also a way that his approach prevents him from authentically relating to himself and others. A helpful reflection considers: What would happen to Matthew if he wrestled with the negative images and expectations culture holds of Black men, along with the accompanying negative treatment, and allowed himself to feel his raw emotions? What would happen to Matthew if he wrestled with his feelings long enough to allow the negative images, expectations, and treatment of Black men to affect him? My assumption is that this might be initially a vulnerable task for Matthew, yet he would discover a more authentic version of himself, one that he and others would recognize as true to the core of his being. In this sense, he would be better able to connect with the core of himself and others with depth as opposed to covering up parts of himself that are, at present, too vulnerable to access. As a result, he would be able to connect deeply with himself and others.

Jamal also described moments when he refused subservient status. He has done so by presenting other (positive) life options for young Black men (instead of the limiting and life-defeating ones present in the media and society). Unlike Matthew, Jamal's description does not express how he personally refuses the negative expectations and assumptions of Black men. Rather, Jamal shared how he tries to get other Black male youth to, in his words, "do better." Jamal noted,

> I just try to bring up other possibilities of things. Uh, just know that you can
> grow up and be, you know, whatever you want to be. Things like that. Try to
> put it, like I said, out on social media, things that I have. I talk about it a lot in
> the shop where I work at. We do bring up a lot of those conversations. Um,
> things like that. I try to tell younger kids some of the things that are going on.

Jamal embodies concern and care for the younger generation of Black men. His response also illustrates that community is an important dimension so that, at the shop where he works, the barbers and other Black men getting haircuts and hanging out have supportive conversations about how to navigate life as a Black man. Jamal's narrative displays that not only does he personally aim to point Black male youth to other life possibilities, but that the community of the barbershop where he works also plays a critical role in facilitating the survival and flourishing of young Black men.

Finally, we can gain additional insight into the process of resisting subservient status by engaging Eddie's narrative on the subject matter. According to his narrative, he refuses subservient status by speaking, writing, and making others aware of the issues facing Black men. He expressed,

> Yeah, I just speak my piece on it and then I leave it at that. But I also want to
> get back to where I'm writing about it. But one of the things I do: I show proof
> in facts to back up what I'm saying. I find sources, I even quote books, quote
> authors. So it's like I'm backing up what I'm saying. I find sources, I even
> quote books, quote authors . . . but it's like I would say my reaction is factual
> and then most other people's reaction is based off of them not knowing and
> their own ignorance.

In this sense, it is important for Eddie to acquire knowledge to back up his spoken and written messages with facts. It has been well chronicled by, particularly, Eddie, Matthew, and Kendrick, along with Black scholars, the importance of knowing oneself and one's own history as a tool to transcend the bondage of racial oppression. While knowing facts alone will not, in itself, lead to liberation, knowing oneself and one's own history is a critically important dimension of psychological liberation from the negative images and expectations of Black men perpetuated by the media and society. When Black men know ourselves, we are less vulnerable to introjecting negative projections from White-dominated culture.

The aforementioned examples have given us access into the psyches of Black men in this book concerning the ways that they have resisted subservient status. While I affirm that Black people might remain as subservient objects in the social order, a la Derrick Bell, I also assert that Black men have the power to resist subservient status, and from such resistance emerges a meaningful and rewarding life. In other words, while society, abiding as it does by the category of race and the workings of racism, will forever perpetuate negative images and expectations of Black men as subservient objects in the social order, Black men can resist these negative images and expectations by using our own agency to define our existence on our own terms in such a way that transcends limitations placed on Black male life by American and global cultures. In this way, a Black man has an opportunity to survive and flourish, even amidst a cultural environment insistent on his demise.

ACKNOWLEDGING OBAMA, ENTERTAINERS, AND SOCIAL ACTIVIST LEADERS

The men in this book recalled and referred to the lives of President Barack Obama along with other leaders and entertainers of the nineteenth, twentieth, and twenty-first centuries as resources for resisting the negative cultural projections aimed at Black men, and the accompanying process of introjection. Specifically, they mentioned Harriet Tubman, Huey Newton, Martin Luther King Jr., Malcolm X, Michael Jordan, Chuck D, Tupac, Mos Def, and Nas, in addition to President Obama. By pointing to these key figures in the cultural milieu, men in this book highlighted the significance that cultural figures have on the mental health of Black men. That is, we can further affirm that culture significantly affects the intrapsychic experiences of Black men.[10] We can infer that these Black men referred to the aforementioned cultural figures for two reasons: 1) To learn from their example; and 2) as a resource to reflect on how these individuals lived amidst the devastating forces of racism. The point here is that political and cultural leaders significantly affect Black men's mental health. Caring for the mental health of Black men, then, includes nurturing political and cultural leaders who will cultivate the survival and flourishing of Black men.

CONCLUSION

This chapter has explored intersubjectivity and considered its impact on the intrapsychic experiences of Black men in this book by considering their: 1) internal emotions of hurt, woundedness, sadness, and the accompanying emotions of frustration and anger; 2) exertion of energy thinking about White people; 3) efforts to resist culture's negative images and expectations of Black men; and 4) tendency to recall and reflect on key figures in culture who function as resources for their mental well-being. Our reflections on the contextual factors impacting the inner lives of Black men is now complete. Part II moves to an explicit introduction and exploration of a Hope to Keep Going framework for care and counseling crafted to care for the mental health of Black men.

NOTES

1. I am referring to the tragic death of a Black man, Erick Garner, who was strangled to death by police after declaring "I can't breathe."

2. As evidenced, in part, by the Ku Klux Klan's endorsement of Donald Trump.

3. bell hooks, *We Real Cool,* xii.

4. hooks, *We Real Cool*, 97.

5. I hold that such a resistance in Black men is both conscious and unconscious.

6. By "they" Jamal means "American society."

7. Nancy McWilliams, *Psychoanalytic Diagnosis: Understanding Personality Structure in the Clinical Process*, 2nd ed. (New York: The Guilford Press, 2011), 111.

8. I am naming that non-Whites can also abide by the ideologies of White-dominated culture through a process of internalized oppression.

9. McWilliams, *Psychoanalytic Diagnosis,* 112.

10. While not the sole focus of this study, I also hold that Black men have power to affect culture. Opportunities for liberating and healing American and global cultures may very well be actualized by acknowledging intersubjective reality. That is, Black men have the power to use our own agency to affect culture.

Part II

A Hope to Keep Going
Framework for Care and Counseling

Chapter Five

Spiritual Hope

"I am because we are."
—Ubuntu Philosophy

"Lifting as we climb."
—The National Association of Colored Women's Clubs

We begin discussion on a Hope to Keep Going framework for care and counseling by exploring spirituality as an essential tool for nurturing hope in Black men. The quotes above characterize spirituality understood through the lens of a traditional West African worldview that values supportive community as a necessary dimension of spirituality, which encourages the well-being of all individuals in community. This worldview and approach to spirituality differs from a Western Eurocentric worldview and approach to spirituality, which privileges individuality—and the flourishing of an individual's spirituality—over the spiritual experiences and needs of others. In fact, some Black Christians have internalized an individualized approach to spirituality which is illustrated by the saying, "As long as I got King Jesus, I don't need nobody else."[1] Such an approach to spirituality is harmful to the well-being of the community because it promotes the flourishing of individuals and minimizes, if not disregards, our relationships with one another. Spirituality must tend to the health of the community (including the ways that we relate to one another), because if communities are not healthy, the most vulnerable and marginalized people suffer. An individualistic approach to spirituality prevents us from considering the ways that our actions affect one another. If one just needs, for example, Jesus (or any other deity) without developing and cultivating life-giving relationships with one another, then spirituality dichotomizes and fragments life. This chapter rejects a dichotomized and fragmented approach to spirituality and proposes a Hope to Keep

Going spirituality that is marked by communal support, an integrated world-view, and respect and reverence for our ancestors.

While religious scholars and theologians have explored the nuances of religion and spirituality, more attention needs to be given by mental health professionals (and all persons caring for the mental health of Black men) to the spirituality of Black men, so that it can function as an effective resource for improving Black men's mental health. There are studies that show spirituality promotes health for Black men, such as Watkins Jr. et al.'s journal article, "The Relationships of Religiosity, Spirituality, Substance Abuse, and Depression Among Black Men Who Have Sex with Men (MSM)" in the *Journal of Religion Health* (2016),[2] which reported that higher spirituality scores equate to less polysubstance abuse and depression. Another study by Namageyo-Funa et al. reported that Black men have used religion and spirituality to cope with living with Type 2 Diabetes.[3] While these and other studies have emerged, there remains a need for additional qualitative research to explore the ways that spirituality can contribute to the mental well-being of Black men so that spirituality can help Black men 1) resist the negative impacts of racism, sexism, classism, and homophobia in our everyday lives; and 2) survive and flourish in the world. This chapter offers my definition of spirituality, reflects on the narratives of Black men in this book (along with narratives in Jeffries IV et al.'s study), considers reflections on Black religion and spirituality by key thinkers, and discusses the presence and potential of a Hope to Keep Going spirituality.

A few fundamental questions guide the flow of this chapter: Is spirituality present in the lives of Black men in this book? If so, in what forms does it appear? Likewise, what are the constructive and destructive elements of spirituality displayed in their lives? How can spirituality function to cultivate the survival, liberation, healing, and flourishing in their lives? And, finally, how might reflection on the spiritual lives of Black men in this book, in dialogue with key thinkers in the study of Black religion and spirituality, inform our understanding of spirituality so that it can function as a helpful resource to cultivate the survival, liberation, healing, and flourishing of Black men?

A DEFINITION OF SPIRITUALITY

As we explore the presence and potential of spirituality in Black men, I first offer my current definition of spirituality. My definition, and this chapter's view on spirituality, does not aim to privilege one particular religious tradition over another. This is not to say that particular religious traditions don't influence the lens that guides the view of spirituality in this chapter. However, the pages within this chapter draw from the narratives of Black men in this book to identify the ways that they perceive, understand, and embody spirituality in order to consider how spirituality can contribute to the survival, liberation, healing, and flourishing of Black men.

Every person reflecting on spirituality does so from a particular vantage point. My vantage point includes experiences teaching at an institution of higher learning, Claremont School of Theology, that values multi-religious dialogue. This means that the ethos of the institution where I teach values conversation on religion and spirituality that acknowledges multiple religious perspectives. However, this is not just an ethos seamlessly woven into the fabric of my institution. Rather, it is also one that I deeply value in my personal and professional life. My first encounter with religious experience and language comes from my early life experiences in a Christian tradition. While Christianity is my initial religious lens, I have sought to embody a multi-religious perspective on faith and spirituality that draws upon various faith traditions throughout the world—I am rooted in Christianity, yet am intentional to dialogue with various religious traditions to consider how spirituality is perceived, conceived, and embodied throughout the world.

Having named my context, I view spirituality as connection with something greater than oneself—a source which extends beyond the wisdom of any one individual. It is something real, yet must be intentionally sought and cultivated for it to become fully realized in an individual's and community's life. That is, while there may be moments when, for instance, the prayers of another person and good intentions of a benevolent being impact the life course of a particular individual or community, one most effectively reaps the benefits of spirituality when one or a community intentionally seeks spirituality. In this sense, there is an element of consciousness raising that occurs when one or a community engages spiritually. Even so, I believe there are moments when the Universe, Spirit, God, and prayers from others work in the favor of an individual, group of people, families, communities, nations, and the world. I believe that spirituality should also improve relationships and is, therefore, concerned with the well-being of all people in the global community. While this is my definition of spirituality, I also believe each person determines the meaning and purpose of spirituality for her or his life. This is significant because when a person, and group of people, have space and agency to determine her or his reality, they are able to attain liberation and healing from destructive external and internal forces. In this sense, spirituality has the power to cultivate liberation and healing in the midst of oppressive social, institutional, and family contexts that would otherwise prevent the survival, liberation, healing, and flourishing of Black men.

Above all, I equate the effects of an integrated spirituality[4] on a person's and community's life with the feeling and experience of ultimate peace. Such a peace faithfully and constructively integrates all of one's or a community's life experiences with integrity. This does not necessarily mean peace without the presence of violence or dissonance. In fact, the effects of striving for liberation often leads to violence[5] simply because people in power never willingly relinquish their power without undergoing a significant process of self-awareness or having their power taken away from them (and people don't like to have power taken away). Rather, no matter what the external reality, spirituality is a one-ness with the soul, nature, the ancestors, and the Universe. It cultivates a spirit of survival, freedom, healing, and wholeness in the lives of spiritual devotees. Spirituality is a gift that can cultivate peace, clarity of thought, and a hope to keep going amidst oppressive forces in the world that have the potential to cause one harm. Without peace, clarity of thought, and hope for a better day, Black men are more prone to self-identify with the negative images and expectations of Black men in the media and society. However, a spirituality of liberation provides Black men with tools to resist negative depictions and expectations of Black men and enables communities and individual Black men to imagine, and re-imagine, Black masculinity in a way that empowers Black men to live free from the life-denying constrains of White supremacy. Spirituality, in this sense, cultivates a liberated consciousness that is formulated by Black people on our own terms in the presence of supportive community. Spirituality taps into the depths of an individual's and a community's soul in ways that a purely psychological understanding of human life cannot. As pastoral theologians have argued, interdisciplinary dialogue between psychology, theology, and cultural studies positions mental health professionals, religious leaders, and all who have an impact on the lives of Black men to care for the depths of Black men's souls.

We have considered, in the previous four chapters, the ways that systemic oppression has negatively affected Black men, and how it has subsequently led to internal and external turmoil in their lives, with negative impacts on the lives of the women in their lives when Black men don't exude empathy or support for the experiences and ambitions of women. This book holds that human flourishing for Black men necessarily includes Black men's developing desire and the ability to extend empathy and support for Black women. Hope to Keep Going spirituality, as offered in this chapter, proceeds with the ethos of communal support for the survival and flourishing of Black women, even as it aims to inspire the same in Black men.

SPIRITUALITY EXPRESSED IN
THE WORDS OF BLACK MEN

We now turn to the spirituality of Black men in this book as articulated in their own words. Their narratives serve as the building blocks for our discussion on the spiritual lives of Black men, and illustrate how they perceive, understand, and embody spirituality. As we consider their words, we can observe that spirituality has four attributes and characteristics in their lives: 1) spirituality as powerful force; 2) spirituality as catalyst for positivity; 3) spirituality as direct knowledge and direct insight; and 4) spirituality as first being observed in another person (e.g., in a mother or grandmother).

They exerted significant energy and passion, quickly responding to questions about society's perception and treatment of them as Black men. However, when I asked them about spirituality, they paused and took additional time to reflect before offering a verbal response. (This is similar to the pause that occurred when they responded to questions about their perspective on what it means to be a woman.) What might be the meaning of this pause and deeper reflection in response to questions on spirituality? I suggest, as one possibility, that the pause illustrates that they had not explicitly reflected on the presence and potential of spirituality in their lives to the degree that they had reflected on the other dimensions of their lives, such as their experience in the world as Black men. It is, therefore, fitting to suggest that spirituality is an under-examined resource in the lives of Black men in this book and that spirituality is a field of inquiry ripe with opportunities to contribute to the mental well-being of Black men.

Six forms of spirituality emerged from our conversations: 1) Prayer and Meditation; 2) Music and Other Art Forms; 3) Connection with Other People, Nature, Ancestors and the Universe; 4) Connection with Self; 5) Moral Compass; and 6) Inspiration and Motivation. These six forms of spirituality are the portals through which Black men in this book accessed spirituality. These six forms of spirituality should not necessarily be viewed in exclusivity. I have simply categorized them separately to provide a way to explore fully each form of spirituality on its own terms. Nonetheless, there are surely points of overlap amongst the six.

Prayer and Meditation

The first form of spirituality explored in this chapter is *Prayer and Meditation*. I link prayer and meditation together because they have similar characteristics. Yet, while similarities exist, differences exist between prayer and meditation in various faith and spiritual traditions. Prayer is a form of communication, often to a deity, in which one or a community expects transcendent intervention in the midst of human situations. Meditation, on the other hand, which can also be conceived as a form of communication, is primarily concerned with communication and connection with self as a way to center oneself in light of an ultimate reality. Recognizing the distinctions and similarities between prayer and meditation, we can explore the ways that prayer and meditation operate in the lives of Black men.

We begin our reflection on prayer and meditation by engaging Matthew's narrative. In the following conversation, Matthew previously expressed that it is important for a man to have a "grand vision" of his life. He continued by saying that the completion of my dissertation was an example of having a grand vision and that our meeting in the Chicago barbershop (where I recruited Black men to participate in this book) was an example of a grand vision. He shared that communication with the spirit led him to "stop in" the barbershop:

> And the spirit helps bring these pieces together, [including] the same way we bonded and merged ourselves in the barbershop effortlessly. Based on me just stopping in checking on my brother-in-law that day. I was just checking in on him. I didn't want anything. I was like, "yo what up brother?" See, the spirit. I was following the spirit. The Spirit told me to go in there and stop in. That's what that was. That was not of my own doing. Not of my own so called conscious doing. But me being in partnership with the Most High allowing the Holy Spirit to lead me.

He later continued,

> when I was cycling across country and . . . needed to stop or needed a place of rest, I didn't know where I was at. I never heard of these sounds before. It was just me and God. And I would pray and say, "Lord, is this a safe place to be?" [God would say] "Yes." I was like, "Ok." That's how I would get direct communication—by prayer, of being out there, by being with him. . . . And so the spirit would be the thing I would follow that would lead me to where I needed to be. . . I always start off the morning with The Lord's Prayer. And that's a regular prayer I say throughout the day to recalibrate. And I feel like this extra energy or aura which is being reinvigorated from within myself that allows me to be able to see externally what I feel inside. That makes my walk even more clear.

We can observe that prayer, for Matthew, provides clarity of thought and guidance. Darrell explicitly named prayer as a form of spirituality in his life when he expressed that "the higher power is there to help and guide when I'm going through certain situations." Matthew's and Darrell's narratives illustrate that prayer is a helpful resource that guides them throughout their lives. This highlights the ability of prayer to guide Black men toward flourishing even when they experience otherwise life-denying forces that threaten their well-being.

As a result of Black men living in a world surrounded by life-denying historical, social, systemic, and institutional forces—particularly as it relates to the high probability of Black men not being understood or extended compassion from others—loneliness can emerge within Black men if they are not surrounded by an affirming group of people and instilled with internal resources to constructively process their life experiences. To this point, Darrell affirms that connection with God is an antidote to loneliness:

when you have God in your life, you're not lonely. Like that helps a lot. . . [My mother] doesn't have a man in her life. You know she's by herself, but she's real spiritual. And she doesn't act like she's lonely. . . . She knows that God is there and she's very spiritual.

While Darrell eventually connected the dots of loneliness to his mother's experiences of loneliness and the ways that spirituality meets this need, his narrative affirms that spirituality, particularly the presence of God, is a faithful companion in life and helps fill the void of loneliness. Spirituality and connection with God as a resource to combat loneliness is significant in the lives of Black men because it can help center Black men emotionally and spiritually in such a way that the negative historical, social, and systemic forces which have the potential to deny Black men don't have the last word. Rather, the faithful companion of a spiritual presence, guiding Black men to peace, healing, and liberation, can function as the ultimate reality and override any negative voices and messages that he receives from the external world. Eddie provides another example of meditation as a form of spirituality. While he does not pray to a particular deity, he expressed, "I don't have to go to church to be spiritual. It's like I can meditate. I can be able to attune myself." While it is unclear what exactly he wants to attune himself with, it is clear that meditation is a way for him to connect with something or a force that he would not have ordinarily connected to without meditation. In this sense, there is an aspect of spirituality that enables a person to connect with a life-giving presence that is not possible without prayer or meditation.

Prayer and meditation also provide Black men with opportunities to express gratitude. Jamal embodies a spirit of gratitude when he prays. While his mother and cousins initially encouraged him to pray early in his life "when bad times come," his current prayer life focuses primarily on gratitude. When asked if spirituality has been useful in his life, Jamal stated,

I mean [it has] when I've had hard times and my mother—who was on drugs—and my older cousins always told me to pray about things when bad times come, or that bad times have helped them. But me personally, I haven't really seen anything other than, like I said, my past. I do thank God through that, and, you know, through just little things, little accomplishments. I always say to myself when I accomplish something big, whether small or, you know, whether big or small. I'ma always take a quick moment just to thank God because I do believe in God . . . I do believe that there is a higher power. . . . I just take that moment to thank [God], and then I keep pushing towards maybe the next thing or continue on with what I'm doing. Other than that, I just feel like if you set your mind to something and you take the proper necessary steps to do so, you should have a great outcome.

In addition to Jamal, Matthew also stated that he likes to thank God for things that happen in his life. He said, "If I wake up and say, 'thank you Lord for allowing me to wake up,' then I know my day is gonna be well no matter what happens." We can observe that extending expressions of gratitude to God is an important dimension of spirituality for Matthew and Jamal. This is essential for cultivating the survival, liberation, and flourishing of Black men because expressions of gratitude are a critical dimension of mental well-being. Developing and maintaining a spirit of gratitude, as an aspect of one's spirituality, can contribute to a Black man's wholeness by strengthening his ability to identify quickly and frequently the blessings in his life in spite of all the chaos that may surround his life. I am thinking of a hymn sung in Black churches where members sing, "Count your blessings. Name them one by one." Gratitude, in the form of a spirituality that sees and gives thanks for one's blessings, helps Black men see and appreciate the blessings in our lives even when we are surrounded by oppressive forces that would otherwise impede our ability to survive and flourish.

Music

A second form of spirituality displayed by Black men in this book is *Music and Other Art Forms*. I am a musician—so one might assume that I naturally listen for the presence of music in people's lives and the ways that it affects their lives. While this is true, Black men in this book pointed to music as an important dimension of their lives without my prompting. Music, as a form of spirituality, provided inspiration and therapeutic relief in the midst of life circumstances. Music is often a resource for emotional healing and engages the affective dimensions of our lives while fostering creative expressions of self and community. All one has to do is turn to John Coltrane's *A Love Supreme*, listen to Billie Holiday singing *Strange Fruit*, or think of the atmosphere at a Jay-Z, Nicki Minaj, or Beyoncé concert to point to and affirm the ways that music captures the soul as a vibrant spiritual experience.[6] Music engages parts of ourselves that purely intellectual pursuits and conversations fail to engage. Too often the arts, and music in particular, are overlooked in scholarly and clinical dialogue. Yet, music therapists and musicologists help us see the important role that music has played throughout history and its continual role in our contemporary lives. Music, as a form of spirituality, provides unique opportunities for Black men to explore the creative and affective dimensions of ourselves while paving new paths to our survival, liberation, healing, and flourishing.

Kendrick told a story of one of his experiences while out at sea with the Navy in which music played a significant role in his life:

> Music really makes me happy. I can tell you this story; and this was the craziest thing. On my first deployment out to sea . . . I listen to my reggae music all the time . . . [Then] my CD came up missing. I flipped out because that's the only thing that kept me . . . I sent out an email . . . I needed that CD

because when you stuck on a ship for three or four weeks at a time with people that's irritating the hell out of you, you almost tempted to push them over in that sea. You almost tempted. . . . That music . . . pretty much saved me from doing anything stupid while I went out to sea. . . . Music. That's the best. I think that's the best therapy. Regardless of how you feelin', you can play your favorite song. I don't care how sad you feel. You can play one of your favorite songs. . . . You may not feel your best, but you'll feel better. Your mother could have just died and you can be like, "Oh I'm depressed [and after listening to music say] Oh, you know what? I feel a little better. I mean my mom dead but you know I feel better." You know? That's it.

I am not sure if Kendrick ever found his CD. However, what is clear from his narrative is that music played a significant therapeutic role in his life by: 1) saving him "from doing anything stupid;" and 2) and helping him to "feel better." A Hope to Keep Going spirituality accomplishes these two tasks in the lives of Black men.

In addition to Kendrick, Eddie affirmed the important role of music in a person's life and explicitly named it as a form of spirituality:

A lot of people don't view music as being spiritual, but if you listen to certain music and they're talking about "oh I'ma go kill this dude," or even with hip hop . . . it's a spirituality. If you listen to music and they talking about, "I just shot this dude. I just cracked these stars. I just robbed somebody and I'm stealing their credit cards" and stuff like that, your mind be like, "yo, let's go do this." . . . If you getting in a state where you angry and say you listen to some music and you upset, you might act out that emotion in that point, based off how you feeling at that point, how you spiritually feeling at that moment.

In this sense, music, as a form of spirituality, has inspirational power to cause one to act in particular ways. The example above points to a way that music can cause someone to act destructively. Yet, we should also observe that while music, as spiritual force, can inspire one to act destructively, it can also inspire one to act creatively and constructively. An example of music, as spirituality, inspiring one to act creatively and constructively is displayed in Eddie's life when music helps him deal with feelings of invisibility. He expressed, "I listen to a lot of music and just try not to flood my mind with negative thoughts or things that are gonna get me upset." In this sense, music helps Eddie counter negative thoughts to prevent him from getting upset. It is, therefore, imperative for mental health professionals, religious leaders, and all people working with Black men to help Black men reflect on the potential, if not already accessed, resource of music in their lives and to explore how it can contribute to our survival, liberation, healing, and flourishing.

Connection with People, Ancestors, and the Universe

We long for loving connection with others. This fact of human relational life is revealed in the lives of Black men in this book. During our conversations, they said that, in addition to the forms of spirituality outlined above, spirituality is also about connecting with other people. For example, Matthew told me that our interview conversation at a restaurant in Hyde Park was a spiritual connection for him. During our conversation, he said, "The spirit is the connectivity for all of it. . . . It's the central conduit for holiness. And holiness is really a connectivity to the whole of it all anyway. It's not being better than thou or greater than you. Holiness is actually being connected to the whole." I asked Matthew what he meant by "the whole." He explained,

> The whole is the universe. . . . The fact that you got things going on in your life. I got things going on in my life. They got things in they life going on. But yet if we don't see how we're part of the commonality, and that point of commonality is the fact that we all want to see the best things happen, not only for ourselves but those who we care about. It's a very universal concept for everyone.

Matthew also mentioned that it is important to have a connection with the ancestors. He elaborated by pointing out that "there are spirits of the ancestors that are still here that seek to be heard." An important dimension of spirituality, therefore, is cultivating connection with the ancestors and ensuring that their voices and life experiences are heard in the ways that we live our contemporary lives. Eddie, referring to the connection he felt between the two of us during our interview conversation said, "I always try to find things that's liberating and interact with people that our spirits can become in tune. Like me and you right now are having a spiritual connection. It's all positivity."

Connection with others, our ancestors, and the Universe is an important aspect of spirituality which can cultivate the survival, liberation, healing, and flourishing of Black men. Living life cut off from these life-giving connections limits our perceptions of reality and Black men's opportunities to survive and flourish in the world. Similarly, living a life that lacks life-giving connection with one's ancestors limits one's ability to appreciate the journeys of our ancestors which contribute to the people that we have become today. Nurturing spiritual practices that create, develop, and maintain positive, affirming, authentic, and life-giving connections with other people, the ancestors, and the Universe position Black men to survive and flourish in the world.

Connection with Self

An important dimension of survival and flourishing in Black men (and for all intents and purposes all humans) consists of maintaining and improving a good relationship with one's self. Having a thriving relationship with one's self enables Black men to be aware of the intricacies of ourselves and the ways that our unique selves can best participate in the world. Spirituality functioned in the lives of Black men in this book as a resource which helps them connect deeply with themselves, especially amidst the oppressive historical, social, and cultural forces impeding their lives. Their narratives demonstrate that they have used spirituality as a way to connect deeply with their unique individual selves. Kendrick explained it this way:

> So people say, "I'm not religious or nothing. I'm spiritual." What does that mean? Like you ask me [and] I don't really know what it means. I just know it's dealing with yourself and how you live your life. So it's your culture. It's your way of life. If you don't know who you are or don't know how to live your life, then your spirit is gonna be bad, cuz you don't know what the hell you doing. . . . But yeah, spirituality is mostly dealing with yourself—how you handle problems.

From Kendrick's narrative, we can gather that spirituality helps a Black man know himself and how to live his life. It also functions as a resource to help a Black man deal with problems as they emerge in life. As Jamal notes, one way that spirituality helps a Black man deal with problems is by helping him to stay calm. He noted, "I think just spirituality could possibly be something just in a calmer manner—just knowing that you can't change anything, so you just take it as it comes, I guess, in a calm sense." Spirituality in this sense helps him experience a sense of calm amidst adversity.

Moral Compass

Black men in this book affirmed that spirituality functions as a moral compass in their lives. Eddie expressed that he "feel[s] like what your morals are and spirituality go hand and hand with each other." Further reflection on a connection between morals and spirituality can affirm that morals, which are often influenced by a person's spirituality, function as a lens through which a person views and interprets the world. From this vantage point, spirituality helps one determine what is right and wrong. Spirituality, as a moral compass, leads a person to develop and maintain particular worldviews—a lens through which to view and interpret reality and the world in which we live. Spirituality, as moral compass, significantly affects one's—and a community's—interpretation of the world in such a way that a person, group, or community of people ascribes value to one way of living and viewing the world over another. In this sense, spirituality, as moral compass, influences how a person makes decisions which necessarily affect the lives of other people. An example of spirituality affecting decision-making includes decisions made by politicians and judges which affect the lives of many people, particularly the most vulnerable and marginalized people of the world. As a result, spirituality as a moral compass is perhaps the form of spirituality that most significantly affects the lives of all people in the global village. Spirituality, as a moral compass, significantly influences our collective human story.

Does spirituality come before morals or do morals precede spirituality? For example, if one embraces homophobic beliefs, do these beliefs stem from one's spirituality or morals? While we can reflect on the relationship between spirituality and morals from the vantage point of seeking to understand homophobic beliefs, we can also reflect on the relationship between spirituality and morals which affirm LGBTQIA persons. Do morals affirming of LGBTQIA persons give birth to a spirituality that is affirming of LGBTQIA persons (an example of morals preceding spirituality)? Or does a spirituality that is affirming of LGBTQIA persons give birth to morals that affirm LGBTQIA persons (an example of spirituality preceding morals)? As illustrated above, Eddie affirmed that spirituality and morals are closely intertwined when he stated that "your morals . . . and spirituality go hand and hand." I agree that there is a close relationship between one's spirituality and moral beliefs, and I am suggesting that religious leaders, mental health professionals, and community leaders working with Black men closely examine the foundations of a Black man's spirituality and morals so that there is congruence between spirituality and morals in such a way that nurtures the liberation of all Black men.

I am probing the relationship between spirituality and morals to examine whether or not there is an inherent homophobic quality about spirituality. Or, can Black men engage spirituality in such a way that affirms, liberates, and heals the emotional experiences and material realities of LGBTQIA persons? I am inclined to believe, whether the oppressive force is racism, sexism, or homophobia (and any other "ism"), that all forms of oppression can use spirituality to further their cause. In this sense, spirituality is not inherently racist, sexist, or homophobic, but it can be used by each of these forms of oppression to further their cause. Because of this reality, it is important to disentangle all forms of oppression from their religious and spiritual roots. People throughout history have used religion and spirituality to advance and support racism, sexism, and homophobia. When religion, spirituality, and faith support racist, sexist, and homophobic ideology, they become dangerous and often unstoppable forces; they become extremely difficult to question because they are held as authoritative directives from God in so much that people believe these directives are God's, the universe's, or the Spirit's ultimate plan for the world. Who can question such an authority? Even so, I hope that those who are on the side of justice and liberation will have the audacity to question any form of oppression, even if it is closely intertwined with religious and spiritual dogma. Yet, religion and spirituality have also been used to spark survival, liberation, and flourishing in the lives of the most vulnerable and marginalized people in the world. In order to nurture the survival and flourishing of Black men, I am suggesting that spirituality must function in a way that is liberating and healing for Black men and all people throughout the world, particularly the most vulnerable and marginalized.

We see the authoritative role of spirituality, as moral compass, displayed in the lives of Black men in this book on the topic of sexuality. Kendrick provides an example of spirituality functioning as a moral compass in his life. During our conversation, he expressed,

> I'm thinking about the gay marriage and all that. People tripping on it. Then I just read something that made a lot of sense. You got two laws. You got man's law and you got God's law. God's law is always going to be there. It's not going to change. Man's law may coincide with God's law and may not. But in the end, it's God's law that's over us. . . in a man's world they say marriage is between whoever. Then the next thing you know, they gonna allow animals to marry. That's man's law. God's law is totally different. . . . If it ain't right, it ain't right. Plain and simple. . . . You got three different religions, the main ones. A lot of them . . . conflict with a lot of stuff. But homosexuality they all agree on and it's wrong.

I asked Kendrick to clarify which three major religions he referred to and he responded: "Islam, Christianity, and Judaism. Those three are pretty much the biggest." What is, perhaps, the most striking in Kendrick's narrative is that he is, essentially, equating gay marriage to animal marriage. In other words, gay marriage is on par with animal activity—it is not even accorded human worth. The implications of such a statement seem obvious—gay marriage should not be considered as an acceptable loving covenant between two people. During our conversation, we did not reflect further on the things that led him to embrace such a stance, but what is clear is that Kendrick invoked religion as an authoritative force to fortify and perpetuate heteronormativity. Kendrick also cited another area of his life in which spirituality functions as a moral guide:

> Spirituality is there to help you make an ethical and moral choice instead of just being out there and deciding to see what happens. Like I had an option when I was in Virginia to go do porn. I said, "Naw, I don't want to do that." I couldn't imagine now going to my son's school and his teacher be like, "I know you. I done seen you a whole bunch of times. What are you doing here?" You know? I didn't want that. If I would have never had any children or if I would have thought that I would never have kids, I probably would have went

with 'em. I make certain decisions based on spirituality. . . . Spirituality helps
me a lot . . . It just makes you think.

Further, alluding to Adam and Eve in the biblical Garden of Eden story,
Darrell said, "I know the woman came from the man because of loneliness;
or just to have that other species with him." Darrell's recounting and interpretation of this religious story leads him to embrace a patriarchal worldview
in which women were created solely for the purposes of meeting a man's
needs. We can now clearly see religious and spiritual roots that contribute to
the worldviews, as illustrated in chapter three, embraced by some Black men
who lack empathy and support for the experiences and ambitions of women.
What is striking about Kendrick and Darrell's narratives is that their resourc-
ing of religion and spirituality fortifies heteronormative, homophobic, and
patriarchal beliefs. In the case of Darrell, we get a sense of how he used a
religious text and doctrine to fortify a worldview that affirms women as
deriving from men and being created for the purpose of meeting men's
needs, namely that of companionship. While it is fitting to care for a Black
man's experiences of loneliness, it is problematic to believe that all women
come from men for the purposes of meeting a man's need for companionship. This ideology has severe consequences on the lives of women and must
be resisted.

Inspiration and Motivation

Our discussion on Black men's spirituality would not be complete without
acknowledging the ways that it has functioned as a source for inspiration and
motivation. Spirituality has the power to nurture hope in the lives of Black
men so that we can keep going in life's journey toward greater freedom,
healing, and flourishing despite the odds and obstacles stacked against us by
oppressive structural and social forces which do anything but motivate and
inspire our survival and ability to thrive in the world. In this sense, the
inspirational and motivational dimensions of spirituality contribute to the
mental health of Black men and prevents nihilism from overtaking our
psyches. Darrell provides an example of spirituality functioning as a source
of hope and motivation:

> I feel like if you have that spiritual reality, if you're spiritual, you . . . have
> something that keeps you motivated. The key word is motivated. That's just
> what it is. It keeps you motivated. Keeps you sane. It gives you hope. It's
> like . . . cuz only man knows so much about this world. . . . We don't know
> how we got here. We know it's some type of higher being, and that's spiritual-
> ity. It's like—it has to be. So that means we have hope to keep going. . . . So I
> think that's what it is. I just defined it—like, motivation.

What a wonderful concept of spirituality to embrace in Black men: motivation that inspires Black men to develop and maintain "hope to keep going." Even if spirituality does not function presently as a source for motivation and inspiration, it can be cultivated in such a way that Black men can develop a way of being and relating to others that maintains hope to keep going, in spite of obstacles. This is no easy feat, yet a spirituality that integrates all of one's life experiences and pushes toward survival, freedom, healing, and flourishing can nurture hope in Black men. In this sense, the well-being of Black men is significantly improved when spirituality is used as a resource to nurture hope to keep going toward the promised land of survival, freedom, healing, and flourishing.

CONSTRUCTIVE AND DESTRUCTIVE
ELEMENTS OF SPIRITUALITY

Having named the forms of spirituality operative in the lives of Black men in this book, it is fruitful to identify the constructive and destructive elements of spirituality present in their lives. By constructive elements of spirituality, I mean the aspects of spirituality which contribute to Black men's survival, liberation, healing, and flourishing. By destructive elements of spirituality, I mean the life-denying aspects of spirituality which cause Black men to become and remain complicit with the oppressive ways that racism, sexism, and homophobia compromise their existence and limit opportunities for human flourishing. Additionally, life-denying aspects of spirituality include all forms of spirituality that encourage Black men to act domineeringly toward others and to maintain lack of concern, empathy, and support for the experiences and ambitions of women. Black men must recognize and cultivate the constructive elements of spirituality in their lives and recognize, resist, and dismantle the destructive elements of spirituality in their lives.

Constructive Elements of Spirituality

What are the constructive elements of spirituality present in the lives of Black men? I'd like to highlight constructive elements of spirituality from each form of spirituality presented above. *Prayer and Meditation* enabled Black men in this book to: access spirituality as a guide and companion, have depth connection with one's self, and have an outlet to express one's gratitude. *Music,* as a form of spirituality, had the ability to make them happy, saved them "from doing something stupid," provided the "best therapy"—making them feel better—and had the power to prevent one's mind from being flooded by negative thinking. *Connection with People, Ancestors, and the Universe* gave them a greater perspective on reality and connected them with the whole of reality dating back to their ancestors. *Connection with Self* fostered deeper knowledge and connection with their own identity and empowered them with wisdom about how to live and deal with adversity. Depth knowledge of self—and connection to self—positions Black men better to survive and thrive no matter what adversity might come their way. Spirituality as *Moral Compass,* when used constructively, inspired Black men in this book to refrain from participating in life-limiting behavior, such as pornography, particularly when considered in light of the effect that it might have on one's child. Lastly, spirituality as *Inspiration and Motivation* has functioned to keep a Black man motivated in the midst of adversity.

Additionally, while it was not evident in more than one of the men in this book, an underrepresented form of spirituality was that of *participating in liberating activity.* Further qualitative research exploring *spirituality as participation in liberating activity* will significantly contribute to our understanding of the presence and potential of spirituality as liberating force in the lives of contemporary Black men. As one of the men in this book noted, "Harriet Tubman got busy!" By this, he meant that participating in liberating activity is an important aspect of spirituality. During a womanist pastoral theology and spiritual care class that I taught at Claremont School of Theology, one of my students shared that she wants her work to focus on "decolonization as spiritual practice." *Participating in liberating activity* as a form of spirituality is consistent with my student's idea of "decolonization as spiritual practice." Specifically, *spirituality as participation in liberating activity* means that one is consistently and actively engaged in activity that liberates the oppressed.

Destructive Elements of Spirituality

While spirituality, as moral compass, can function as a positive resource for the mental well-being of Black men, it can also function destructively when it perpetuates homophobic, heteronormative, and sexist worldviews, as we have witnessed in the narratives above. Therefore, while spirituality as moral compass has the potential to have a positive impact on the lives of Black men and those in our relational world, it is also the form of spirituality that can cause, perhaps, the most destruction in the world. Spirituality in the form of music can also function destructively if it is composed and performed from the grounds of hegemony, sexism, racism, classism, homophobia, heteronormativity, and any other oppressive ideology. If spirituality is to be used to cultivate the survival, liberation, healing, and flourishing of Black men and the most vulnerable and marginalized people in the world, it must proceed without embracing oppressive sentiments.

FRAGMENTED SPIRITUALITY

What might it look like to place the narratives of Black men in this chapter in dialogue with key thinkers who have written on Black religion and spirituality? The next section does just that by exploring the works of Almeda Wright, Lee Butler Jr., Jeffries IV et al., and Anthony Pinn. To begin, we see fragmented spirituality illustrated in Eddie's dialogue on a slave master and slave praying to the same God. Eddie said, "I grew up in the church, but my viewpoints on religion is [that] it's passed on from the oppressor and slave master . . . how can we have a master and the slave pray to the same God? It's backwards. So it's like, that's my struggle." Eddie's thought process displays the dilemma that Black men, with similar experiences and reflections, have concerning the usefulness of spirituality in their lives. Certainly, we can understand how contradictory spirituality might seem if a slave owner and a slave are praying to the same God. As a result, it can be easy for Black men to give up on spirituality as a useful tool for improving their lives if they see their oppressor praying to the same God while perpetuating oppression. It is clear that the slave owner is not praying to a God of liberation. The prayers of the slave owner are not concerned with liberating slaves nor other oppressed people. The slave owner affirms and preaches individual piety as the true marker of spirituality, a spirituality that is not concerned with liberating the oppressed. Such a spirituality, which is not grounded in a concern for liberation and social justice, is a trademark of fragmented spirituality. However, Black men can embody an integrated spirituality that speaks to their experiences in the world if they see and experience other forms of spirituality that are concerned with liberation from all forms of oppression in the world.

Almeda Wright

We all have multiple life experiences in the world dating back from our birth to the present. If we are not intentional about acknowledging and integrating all of our life experiences, we are apt to fragment our experiences in the world. Wright affirms that fragmentation serves a purpose, and for our purposes, we can observe that fragmentation serves a psychological purpose in helping a person function emotionally amidst the many different experiences he or she has in the world. Yet, while fragmentation can be understood by Western-dominated thinkers in psychological terms, Wright helps us grapple with fragmented spirituality and names that it is "highly functional."[7] Wright observes ways that African American Christian youth in her study engaged spirituality as a way to forward their personal success without integrating spirituality as a tool to spark social liberation. She notes that,

> Fragmented spirituality helps youth function in a society where individualism is rampant and absolute truths are not part of the contemporary lexicon . . . African American Christian youth . . . have positive outlooks on their personal success, based on their personal relationship with Jesus. Many of these youth passionately respond that they can do "all things through Christ who strengthens them" and do not find it contradictory to exclude working toward social and systemic change in the list of "all things." . . . At the other end of the spectrum, I have also encountered African American Christian youth who are actively engaged in their communities, even as social activists . . . but who also do not see this work as remotely connected to a larger history of Christian social witness or to any Christian community.[8]

Wright states that "the African American community and church are at risk if they perpetuate youth participation in the mythology that the personal and the communal are separate; or that the spiritual and political are separate."[9] From this vantage point, fragmented spirituality separates personal experience from social experience.

Wright goes on to observe that "fragmented spirituality is problematic and that youth should work to embrace an *integrating spirituality*."[10] She further states the following,

> Integrating spirituality is spirituality that empowers youth to hold together the seemingly disparate areas of their lives, to tap into the resources of their faith communities and learn from historical and current faith exemplars, in order to see themselves as capable of living abundant life by effecting change on individual, communal, and systemic levels.[11]

I agree with Wright's decree that fragmented spirituality is problematic and affirm that Black men can benefit from embracing, embodying, and cultivating a spirituality that fully integrates all of their life experiences. Wright notes that,

> Spirituality then, by definition, should offer openness to the holding together of the complexities of their lives and not simply a condemnation of the diversity. What is problematic is not that youth or adults experience fragmentation, but rather the problem emerges when they are unable to faithfully navigate the fragments of their lives.[12]

Spirituality in the lives of Black men must integrate all of our life experiences. This means that Black men's experiences of being chronically disrespected, disregarded, discredited, feared, and devalued—as well as those of joy, gratitude, and celebration—must be taken seriously in our religious and spiritual practices to cultivate the survival, liberation, healing, and flourishing of Black men. Likewise, Black men's tendency not to have empathy or support for the experiences and ambitions of women, as illustrated in this book, needs to be addressed and critiqued as part of an integrated spirituality.

In order to debunk fragmented spirituality, it is helpful to understand factors contributing to it. Wright names two contributing factors to fragmented spirituality: the privatization of religion and American individualism. Concerning the first, Wright notes that theories of privatization of religion "point to ways that many segments of modern society expected and fostered religions, particularly institutions and communities, to remain separate from and not to affect political and systemic change."[13] To the second contributing factor to fragmented spirituality, Wright names the ways that American individualism has impacted religious life. She notes,

> American individualism helps us explore the larger sociological context in which fragmentation occurs, in that American individualism goes hand in hand with the tendencies of postmodern youth to practice and express religious convictions that are primarily concerned with individual and personal themes.[14]

This way of being spiritual limits not only postmodern youth, but also Black men's ability to use spirituality as a resource for survival and flourishing in the context of life-giving community. Embracing spirituality that is dictated by American individualism prevents Black men from caring for other people and from caring enough to resist systemic oppression that affects others.

William Jeffries IV, Brian Dodge, and Theo Sandfort

In a study analyzing qualitative interviews of twenty-eight bisexual Black men living in New York City, William Jeffries IV, Brian Dodge, and Theo Sandfort state that,

> Traditionally, religion has been a major source of institutional support and well-being for Black people in the USA. However, when juxtaposed against sexuality, religion's positive effect upon the lives of non-heterosexual individuals is questionable. Research suggests that non-heterosexuals often abandon structured religion for spirituality due to the homonegativity perpetuated through religious institutions.[15]

Like Victor Anderson's position of acknowledging difference, I am advocating for Black spirituality to acknowledge difference among Black men, particularly in regards to sexuality. There are four themes I raise from the empirical findings in Jeffries IV et al.'s study that will be helpful for our reflections on the spiritual lives of Black men. Two of them are named in this section on *Fragmenting Spirituality* and the other two are named under the next section, *Integrating Spirituality*, as they fit under each of these categories, respectively. The first point raised as an example of fragmented spirituality concerns *religious institution's intolerance of bisexuality* as reported by the bisexual Black men in Jeffries et al.'s study.

> Fifteen participants unequivocally spoke of their bisexuality being unaccepted by their religious communities. No participants spoke of condemnation that they received for having non-marital heterosexual sex. All of their condemned sexual relations were those that were with other men. When asked if they were able to openly discuss their sexuality within the context of religion, participants provided remakes like "I can't talk to them about it" or "I know that would be an issue there."[16]

One twenty-seven-year-old Black male participant in Jeffries et al.'s study noted that it is scary to think of revealing his bisexuality to his Islamic faith community. He felt that he wouldn't be respected anymore and that his life would be in jeopardy if his religious community discovered his bisexuality.[17]

We can note that this points to the reality that for many religious institutions and communities of faith, sexuality must be kept hidden. This reality is supported by Jeffries et al.'s findings that participants in their study "felt they had to go to great lengths to keep their sexuality hidden from their religious communities."[18] Jeffries et al. reported that bisexual Black male participants were also told that they were going to hell for their bisexuality. They also experienced condemnation from their mothers for being bisexual. Because of these factors, Jeffries et al. assert that there are unique stressors in the lives of Black bisexual men as a result of experiences in their faith communities that have been intolerant of their bisexuality. Additionally, Jeffries et al. cited participants in their study who said that religious leaders tried to convert them to heterosexuality. This begs the question: Can religious leaders and communities engage LGBTQ persons without trying, or wanting, to convert them to heterosexuality?

The second theme I point to from Jeffrey et al.'s study is *spiritual convictions and moral responsibilities*. Black men in Jeffries et al.'s study displayed that moral responsibilities are based on their spiritual convictions. Participants who provided data on this theme shared that their vision, as spiritual people, is to be in a monogamous heterosexual marriage. They felt that being married to a woman was the Christian thing to do. One participant noted that being a Christian father meant being in fidelity with his wife in a heterosexual marriage. He expressed,

> I mean, it's just the way I look at it. I mean, it's my opinion . . . do this stuff [sex with men and women] before you get married. Because I'm in church, you're making a promise before God, and I just can't (laughter) . . . certain things you got to stop. You know, you get to a point where you want it to stop, enough is enough. And that's why I say, when I get married and make my kids, you know, it's going to have to be strictly straight. . . . I'm in a leadership

role, and I want to be a positive role model, and I got young people looking up to me. [19]

From this participant's narrative, we can ask the question: Must a man be heterosexual in order to be looked up to by young people in the church? Jeffries et al. note that there were no participants in their study who believed that they could be a leader or role model while also being bisexual. Therefore, caregivers, mental health professionals, and leaders that cultivate spirituality in Black men should consider how to shape a different vision of spirituality so that Black men's spiritual convictions, while embodying responsible behavior, also makes space for someone who is non-heterosexual to be viewed as an upstanding leader and role model in families, faith communities, and the larger society.

INTEGRATED SPIRITUALITY: SURVIVAL, RESISTANCE, CREATIVITY, AND THE QUEST FOR COMPLEX SUBJECTIVITY

How might we envision spirituality for contemporary Black men in such a way that resists fragmented spirituality and embraces integrated spirituality? I view an integrated spirituality as a helpful resource for cultivating the mental wellbeing of Black men. As a way to counter the privatization of religion and American individualism, Wright argues that "an embrace or rethinking of the role of religion in communal and public life is . . . essential and possible within contemporary US culture."[20]

Wright offers a proposal to counter fragmented spirituality. There are three points from her proposal that I highlight because of their ability to aid our efforts to care for the mental health of Black men. The first point is derived from her reference to Monica Coleman's *Making a Way Out of No Way* or creative transformation. If Black men cultivate an audacity within to "make a way out of no way" in spite of the negative forces impeding our lives, we have the ability to survive and thrive. Second, Wright's theme of *Conversion to the Neighbor: Spirituality of Liberation* helps Black men commit ourselves to our neighbors and to do whatever we can to help liberate our neighbors from the grips of oppression. Wright cites Gutierrez who argues that "'To be converted means to commit oneself to the process of the liberation of the poor and oppressed, to commit oneself lucidly, realistically, and concretely . . . with an analysis of the situation and a strategy for action.'"[21] The third theme is *Hope—Desire and Expectation.* Wright notes that, according to Mary Townes, hope is the "combination of desire and expectation."[22] This theme of *Hope—Desire and Expectation* is central to the Hope to Keep Going framework of care and counseling offered in this book. Embracing hope, which includes desire and expectation, is also key for countering nihilism in Black men who might, otherwise, feel hopeless while living in a world and local communities that are not interested in tending to the pertinent issues necessary to address their survival, liberation, healing, and flourishing. Yet, an embrace of spirituality which maintains a desire and expectation for good things to happen in one's life and the lives of other marginalized, vulnerable, and oppressed people, helps Black men develop and maintain a hopeful outlook on life, as they desire and expect a better day for the present and future. Ultimately, Wright helps us understand fragmented spirituality and offers ways to counter it with an integrated vision of spirituality that can nurture the flourishing of Black men.

Integrated spirituality is the ideal form of spirituality affirmed in this book and is the essence of a Hope to Keep Going spirituality which inspires and nurtures survival, liberation, healing, and flourishing in Black men. An important dimension of this type of spirituality consists of taking seriously the relationships that we have with one another and the relationships we have with the larger social world. A Hope to Keep Going spirituality, therefore, improves relationships between people and resists the urge to fragment personal faith from life-giving relationships with others. This view of spirituality emerges from the viewpoint that human relationships matter. As such, a Hope to Keep Going spirituality improves relationships. While it is important for a Hope to Keep Going spirituality to cultivate healthy relationships with the divine and our inner selves, it must also take seriously improving relationships with other people so that our human relationships flourish as life-giving sources of strength which can empower us to keep going to realize greater justice, peace, liberation, healing, and human flourishing in the world for all people, and particularly for the most vulnerable. A Hope to Keep Going spirituality embraces the worldview that all people, considered our sisters and brothers in the human village, are of sacred worth and, accordingly, should be cherished and treated as such. By "sacred" I mean a deep valuing and respect for all people and the relationships we have with one another.

Anthony B. Pinn

Black religious institutions in the United States have historically tended to the spiritual lives of Black people and Blacks' relationships with U.S. society and the larger world. I raise the perspectives and worldviews of Black religious institutions because it is short-sighted to consider the spiritual lives of Black men without acknowledging the ways that spirituality has functioned in Black religious institutions.[23] It is important to consider the spirituality that has guided religious institutions because religious experiences and spirituality in religious institutions have, at least to some degree, influenced the ways that Black men in this book, and their families, have understood, conceived, and embodied spirituality. As previously mentioned, this chapter seeks to understand and reflect on spirituality in the contemporary lives of Black men without limiting our focus to any one particular religious tradition. With this perspective in mind, the following section engages Anthony Pinn's reflections on Black religion and investigates the ways that religion and spirituality have functioned in Black religious institutions. I use Pinn's concept of complex subjectivity as a framework to understand the essence of Black spirituality and its potential for cultivating survival, liberation, healing and human flourishing in Black men.

Acts of Terror & Rituals of Reference

Pinn reflects on acts of terror enacted upon[24] Black people in the United States, including auctions and lynchings, and explores the ways that Black religion and spirituality have responded to acts of terror which have objectified and dehumanized Black people. Pinn observes that

> for slaves and their descendants, rituals of reference such as auctions and lynchings fostered a form of terror or dread by reinforcing and celebrating blacks' status as objects . . . the sense of terror or dread promoted by these rituals gave rise to the historical manifestations of religiosity . . . I argue that this dread sparks the development of practices, doctrines, and institutional structure earmarked for historical liberation from terror.[25]

Pinn further observes that "rituals of reference reinforce a fixed identity as object; recognition of this status fosters a form of dread or terror; and religion manifested in black life is a response to or wrestling against this terror, understood in terms of liberation."[26] One of the ways that Black religion, and for our purposes, Black spirituality, has functioned in the lives of Black people, therefore, is as a response to terror, while also helping Black people strive for and, in many instances, achieve liberation. Spirituality from this vantage point resists any worldview that objectifies and dehumanizes Black men. A Hope to Keep Going spirituality, therefore, maintains a defiant spirit to resist any attempt to objectify and dehumanize Black men and considers survival, liberation, healing, and human flourishing as its primary concern.

While Black religion and spirituality respond to acts of terror enacted upon Black people, Pinn observes that Black religion is not solely concerned with reacting to terror. Rather, Black religion encompasses a healthy tension between reactivity and creativity. Pinn notes,

> Black religion is more than just a move against white actions; because they entail an evolving tension between reaction and creativity, black religious forms are not simply dependent on and reflective of white life. In fact, the survival of various forms of black religion, and the development of others, is

premised upon a tradition's ability to adapt and adjust to the changing nature
of attack on black humanity.[27]

In the spirit of creativity, a Hope to Keep Going spirituality not only affirms
the need to resist oppression in a Black man's life. Rather, such a spirituality
also exudes a *creative* dimension to imagine and strive for, in Pinn's words,
"something more" in life.

Given Black spirituality's ability to function as a helpful resource for
cultivating the mental well-being of Black men—through its ability to inspire
and nurture a spirit of resistance and creativity—it is fitting to reflect on the
barriers that have been erected to prevent Black people from tending to their
spiritual needs. To this point, Pinn points out that "[s]lave owners were
reluctant to give sustained attention to the spiritual needs of blacks because
they believed such attention would ultimately produce rebellions and a general weakening of important social arrangements."[28] This historical occurrence is significant in that it helps us ask the question: To what degree are the
spiritual needs and spirituality of Black men not engaged because people
operating in positions of power fear that spirituality could lead Black men to
have greater courage, vision, and strength to rebel against and triumph over
systemic, cultural, and institutional oppression? Or, are the spiritual needs of
Black men not engaged because of a lack of awareness of the liberating and
healing power of Black spirituality? Or, could the reason also be a result of a
lack of awareness that spirituality has the power to propel Black men to
embody and exude greater courage, vision, and strength to rebel against and
triumph over oppressive systems, cultures, and institutions? Pinn's reflections on slave owners' reluctance to tend to the spiritual needs of Black
people demonstrate that slave owners were, indeed, aware that spirituality
possessed the power to cultivate a spirit of rebellion and, consequently, to
achieve freedom for Black men. This is a positive dimension of spirituality
that must not be pathologized or overlooked and can help Black men rebel
against oppressive cultures, systems, and institutions and, ultimately, dismantle social structures that cause Black men to be objectified and dehumanized. An integrated spirituality, consistent with a Hope to Keep Going framework for care and counseling, resists the objectification and dehumanization
of Black men and strives for something more—something more life-giving—
for the lives of Black men and the people in their world.

A Hope to Keep Going spirituality, therefore, equips Black men to see
oppression clearly and to rebel against it with every fiber of their being. This
includes seeing and rebelling against oppressive cultures, systems, institutions, and relationships that prevent Black men from surviving and experiencing liberation, healing, and human flourishing. With an unwavering eye
focused on liberation, a Hope to Keep Going spirituality identifies, decon-
structs, and dismantles oppressive norms so that Black men can have the

opportunity to survive and flourish in life. For these reasons, religious leaders, therapists and community leaders should integrate spirituality as a helpful resource for cultivating the survival, liberation, healing and human flourishing of Black men. Ignoring a Hope to Keep Going spirituality that maintains an ethic of liberation as its starting point is akin to participating in the same practice of slave owners who sought to prevent Black people from accessing spirituality because of its power to liberate, heal, and cultivate human wholeness in their lives during slavery. Providing care for Black men without using the life-giving resources of Black religion and spirituality is a missed opportunity to cultivate the survival, liberation, healing, and human flourishing of Black men. It is, therefore, wise to reflect on the history of Black religion and spirituality, which has fostered survival, liberation, healing, and human wholeness[29] in Black people, and to assess the degree to which U.S. society and Black communities are using the liberating and healing resources of Black religion and spirituality to promote the mental well-being of Black men. Black religion and spirituality were relentless and defiant in their pursuit of freedom! So, too, must be our theories and practices of care, counseling, and community leadership with Black men. While a Hope to Keep Going spirituality strives for liberation, it also acknowledges the pain experienced by Black people and tends to the need for spirituality to nurture and foster emotional healing in individuals and communities. Rituals and other elements of spirituality have the power to foster emotional healing in Black men who have experienced and continue to experience acts of terror upon their lives.

Black Churches and The Nation of Islam

Let's take a moment to consider how Black religious institutions such as Black churches and the Nation of Islam have influenced the spirituality of Black people. Pinn observes that "[l]iberation from the vantage point of the Black Church revolves around a transformation of existing relationships, both physical and spiritual."[30] This ethos of liberation revolving around transformation of relationships aligns well with my view that spirituality must positively transform human relationships. One of the significant ways that transformation can occur in Black men's relationships with other people and the larger social environment is by recognizing their agency, activating it, and living fully into it to craft a better life for themselves and the people in their world, which should necessarily include Black women. By activating their own agency, Black men can craft a better future for their lives, as opposed to giving in to the negative expectations of themselves projected onto them by the outside world. To the point of agency, Pinn notes that "[t]he Black church as a manifestation of religion responds to terror by seeking to establish blacks as agents of will."[31] Living as agents of will is significant for the mental well-being of Black men because it normalizes an approach to life that maintains as a chief aim willing a more positive existence rather than giving into negative expectations of the external world.

In addition to reflection on Black Christianity, Pinn reflects on Islam in the Black community and identifies three aspects of liberation found in the Nation of Islam: "(1) religion as institutional reality wrestling against socioeconomic and political dependence; (2) aesthetic and ritual dimensions of religion as liberation; and (3) ethics and religious thought as liberation."[32] We see again Black religion and spirituality, in this case The Nation of Islam, encouraging Black people to live as agents of will. The Nation of Islam was concerned with advocating for its adherents to live as agents of will socioeconomically, politically, and morally. Minister Louis Farrakhan of the Nation expressed it this way:

> Without the will to make sacrifices the country will go down. The rich have to be imbued with that spiritual and moral desire to sacrifice more of their profits to help America survive.[33]

Spiritual awakening, therefore, leads to a moral consciousness that rejects greed while promoting a spirit of sacrifice to achieve liberation, particularly for the most vulnerable, marginalized, and oppressed in U.S. society. Spirituality, as Farrakhan envisioned it—and as embraced in a Hope to Keep Going framework for care—must, therefore, cultivate resistance to sexism, classism, racism, White supremacy, and Black inferiority, and, I add, resistance to homophobia.

Taking a cue from Pinn's theory of religion, a Hope to Keep Going spirituality wrestles with dehumanized treatment of Black men and does not accept it as the final word. A Hope to Keep Going spirituality exudes creativity, as evident in art, which enables Black people to live as agents of will. In his chapter, "'I'll Make Me A World'—Black Religion as Historical Context," Pinn describes the importance of the arts and writes, "through art blacks find themselves as they are and as they wish to be."[34] Art is a tremendously valuable resource for helping Black people develop and maintain agency by providing a way for Blacks to identify accurately our experiences in the world while creatively painting a picture of what we want to become in it. Through this creative process, Black people can become who we want to be without yielding to the negative and false depictions of ourselves presented in the media and society.

PASTORAL THEOLOGICAL AND PSYCHOTHERAPEUTIC IMPLICATIONS OF COMPLEX SUBJECTIVITY

Our reflections on Pinn's thought have led us to this point to consider how his concept of complex subjectivity can improve the mental health of Black men. Pinn suggests that "an understanding of religion as historical manifestation of a struggle for liberation embedded in culture does not fully capture the nature and meaning of black religion."[35] Rather, "there is a deeper and more central concern resting behind such historical expressions as the Black Church and the Nation of Islam."[36] Pinn labels this central concern the *quest for complex subjectivity*. Complex subjectivity entails a person taking agency to move from being an "object controlled by oppressive and essentializing forces"[37] to living "with a complex and creative identity."[38] Acknowledging one's complex identity and developing one's creative identity in the context of life-giving community enables one to acknowledge the diversity of her or his life experiences and, in turn, live faithfully as an authentic person, integrating all of her or his life experiences. I contend that the quest for complex subjectivity is a unique attribute of spirituality that purely psychological understandings of the personality[39] do not fully explore. Fully exploring the quest for complex subjectivity can open up creative and constructive possibilities for Black men's survival, liberation, healing, and flourishing. Developing and maintaining commitments to exploring an "expanding range of life options and movements"[40] is essential for those caring for Black men, and for Black men themselves, particularly because of the prevalence of negatives images and expectations of Black men in the media and society. Commitment to spirituality that maintains a quest for complex subjectivity helps Black men desire and expect more from life, creatively and constructively.

REFLECTIONS ON STOMP THE YARD

Black religious thinkers like Pinn and Wright help us consider the communal nature of Black religion and spirituality, as well as its integrative nature, which does not split "sacred" and "secular" experience. According to this view of spirituality, all of life is sacred and should be treated as such. Relating to one another as if we are all sacred means that we relate to one another with a spirit of community and, accordingly, see everyone as family, rooting and cheering for the survival and flourishing of everyone in the human family. An African view of spirituality takes seriously the cultivation of human relationships as exemplified in the phrases "I am because we are" and "Lift as we climb." With this view of spirituality in mind, I conclude this chapter with a contemporary example of spirituality in the lives of Black men as

exemplified in Black gangs and fraternities. I raise these examples to illustrate that a communal and integrative model of spirituality and care already
exists in Black gangs and fraternities and should be considered in any model
of care concerned with the mental well-being of Black men.

While Black gangs might be viewed negatively because of their perceived
or real destructive impacts on Black communities and society-at-large, the
argument I make here, and also made previously by others, is that there is a
collective spirituality of Black gang life in which gang members care for one
another. Similarly, members of Black fraternities are supportive of one another. There is an embedded spirituality in gang and fraternity life, particularly through their concern to care deeply for one another, which is evidence of
the presence of a communal nature of care that is nurtured by a Hope to Keep
Going spirituality. While an in-depth discussion of Black gang and fraternity
life is beyond the scope of this book, I take a moment here to highlight a few
aspects of Black fraternity life as exemplified in the film *Stomp the Yard* that
can help us better care for the mental health of Black men in context of
supportive community as a vital dimension of spirituality which considers an
individual's identity and personhood in positive and affirming relationship
with the whole community.

There are two points I raise from the film *Stomp the Yard* that can aid our
ability to care for the mental health of Black men. The first point focuses on
the communal support that steppers of the fraternities in the film received
during step shows from members in the audience. The second point focuses
on the experience and support of brotherhood exemplified during a fraternal
initiation ceremony. To the first point, viewers of the film *Stomp the Yard*
encounter a scene where the audience at a step show cheers on all the steppers with wild enthusiasm. The steppers, who are members of the fraternities,
are supportive of one another and are enthusiastically cheered on by the
audience that surrounds the steppers performing on the stage. This demonstrates the communal nature of care nurtured by Hope to Keep Going spirituality. This scene not only demonstrates a communal nature of care, it also
affirms a view of spirituality that does not split "sacred" and "secular" experience. This is illustrated during the step show when the brotherhood of
steppers sings the gospel song, "I Got a Feeling [that everything's gonna be
alright]," just before breaking out to sing M. C. Hammer's "Can't Touch
This." I raise this example to illustrate that spirituality in the lives of Black
men must encourage and nurture supportive life-giving brotherhoods and
resource all constructive dimensions of Black cultural life, such as the wisdom found in "sacred" songs such as "I Got a Feeling" and "secular" songs
such as M.C. Hammer's "Can't Touch This," to care for the mental health of
Black men. The second point I raise from *Stomp the Yard* references an
initiation ceremony where pledgees of a fraternity march into an initiation
ceremony, supported by members of the community, chanting, "We got to

keep pushing, We got to keep moving, we got to keep fighting, Ohhhh brother! We got to keep pushing, We got to keep moving. We almost there!" This chant is fitting for the Hope to Keep Going framework of care offered in this book. After the pledgees march into the ceremony with hoodies on (to cover their heads and conceal their individual identity until the time of revealing), they come to a halt surrounded by the cheers and applause of the crowd. The pledgees then introduce themselves individually (still with affirmative applause and cheering from the audience). Next, they collectively hold their heads up together with pride and remove their hoodies. The crowd continues to cheer them on with enthusiasm. After revealing themselves as a unit, they each step forward from the unit of brothers to introduce themselves individually with support from the community. As each pledgee introduces himself, he is cheered on by the crowd. While *Stomp the Yard* is a film depicting Black fraternal life, and therefore might miss some of the nuances of Black fraternities, it points to a spirit of brotherhood, communal support of brotherhood, and support for individual Black men within that brotherhood. This spirit of communal support and care can aid our abilities to care for the mental health of Black men.

AFFIRMING SEXUAL ORIENTATION AS A CRITICAL DIMENSION OF HOPE TO KEEP GOING SPIRITUALITY

While we have considered helpful aspects of an integrated Hope to Keep Going spirituality which fosters communal support and does not split "sacred" and "secular" experience, it is also critical to acknowledge that Hope to Keep Going spirituality aims to affirm fully persons identifying as LGBTQIA. Hope to Keep Going spirituality contributes to the survival, liberation, healing, and flourishing of LGBTQIA people. Earlier in this chapter, I identified two themes from the Jeffries et al. study that displayed fragmented spirituality. I now take a moment to highlight two themes from their study that display aspects of an integrated spirituality. The first of the two themes is *using spirituality to validate themselves as bisexual Black men.* Jeffries et al. note that the participants in their study made a distinction between religion and spirituality. The participants resonated more deeply with spirituality and affirmed that spirituality encompasses their own faith and relationships with God or the divine. Jeffries et al. note that the Black male participants in their study "often questioned sanctions touted by organized religious entities and, in the face of religious condemnation, used spirituality to validate themselves as bisexual men."[41] The following narrative displays how a nineteen-year-old participant in Jeffries et al.'s study reflected on his bisexuality in light of his view of God:

I think that [God] knows, because . . . well a lot of times, people don't let me be gay. Like, you know what I'm saying? Like, God, can I wake up tomorrow, just don't like boys anymore? But it doesn't never happen. And, you know, I tried to, make some sense in my head, and it's that the solution I came up with is that he knows, and he knows that I can't control it, and that he knows what's going on. I mean, he has to accept that, because, I mean, like, why would he not like me, and why would he want to send me to Hell, if I can't control this feeling, and I want to do it, and if I can't do it, I'm going to be unhappy?[42]

This Black man used his own resourcefulness constructively to imagine a God who loves him as he is and has compassion for his lived experiences. He is so resourceful that he can resist any temptation to accept blindly the condemnation that he might receive from some religious leaders and other people in his world who would, otherwise, condemn him for being a bisexual Black man. He reflects critically on God as a loving God and, in the process, is able to imagine himself as loved by God and accepted as a bisexual Black man. His ability to draw from his own life experiences and reflect critically from the vantage point of his own experience is important for cultivating, developing, and maintaining a life-giving spirituality for gay and bisexual Black men.

The second theme from the Jeffrey et al. article that is helpful for an integrated Hope to Keep Going spirituality is *using spirituality to deal with hurt*. Jeffries et al.'s study points out that a twenty-four-year-old bisexual Black man revealed that God helped him deal with the disappointment of not becoming a father due to an abortion obtained by his cohabiting partner. He expressed,

Yeah, I wanted another baby. She actually had, she had gotten pregnant, but she got an abortion. (So you wanted a baby and she had an abortion?) Yeah. (How did that make you feel?) I was hurt, I was hurt. I just brushed it off because I just thought . . . I guess it wasn't my time. I guess God, I just thought God said it wasn't my time to be a father right now. Or, maybe she wasn't the right person. You know. But I was hurt. I tried to play like [I] wasn't hurt. But I was hurt. But, then still . . . in way, I'm thankful because she's just not a right mother.[43]

This narrative points to hurt as a very important emotional experience of Black men that a Hope to Keep Going spirituality has the opportunity to address. When engaging spirituality to care for Black men, we should ask ourselves if the spirituality acknowledged the hurt experienced by Black men? In the case of gay and bisexual Black men, does spirituality address their hurt in life-giving ways? Before religious leaders, mental health practitioners, and all persons working with Black men can adequately resource spirituality as a way to help Black men, we must first acknowledge the hurt and discern the nuances of the hurt experienced by Black men. Spirituality must, therefore, tend to the hurt experienced by gay and bisexual Black men (and all Black men) in order to foster healing and provide support. Hope to Keep Going spirituality fosters healing and provides support while helping Black men make constructive meaning of their life experiences to make the best decisions to live a better life in the present and into the future.

THE PRESENCE AND POTENTIAL OF HOPE TO KEEP GOING SPIRITUALITY IN THE LIVES OF BLACK MEN

To cultivate spirituality in Black men that leads to survival, liberation, healing, and flourishing, a Hope to Keep Going spirituality explicitly helps Black men reflect on the following questions: 1) How are you actively resisting White supremacy?; 2) How are you actively resisting sexism?; 3) How are you actively resisting heteronormativity and homophobia?; 4) How are you making meaning in life?; 5) In what ways are you taking agency in your life?; 6) What more do you want out of life?; 7) How can you integrate all your life experiences in a meaningful and life-giving way?; 8) Are you in touch with the spirit, life experiences, and stories of your ancestors?; 9) How does your awareness of your ancestors inform the way that you live your life in the present and into the future?; and 10) What support do you need to survive and flourish? These questions help those who care for the lives of Black men, and Black men ourselves, reflect on life in such a way that leads to an integrated Hope to Keep Going spirituality which can help Black men survive and flourish in the United States and larger world.

Reflection on the narratives of Black men in this book leads me to make the argument that communities and religious leaders, scholars, counselors, and families should work to foster constructive life-affirming spirituality in their lives as a way to resist oppression, survive, and achieve liberation, healing, and flourishing. I have intentionally refrained from naming one particular religious tradition as the ideal one for cultivating a constructive Hope to Keep Going spirituality for Black men. Rather, I take the approach that a variety of spiritual and faith traditions can foster constructive live-affirming spirituality that can be beneficial for the mental well-being of Black men. I also made this move because I wanted to leave the spirit of creativity open to you, the reader, to discern which religious and spiritual traditions and practices, including the possibility of new ones, might optimally spark constructive life-affirming spirituality for Black men. In this spirit, various forms of inner journey work and rituals—including communal gatherings—can catapult constructive life-affirming spiritual practices into the flourishing of Black men. Mental health therapists can reflect—along with Black male clients—to determine whether or not theological beliefs and spirituality have a constructive or destructive impact in their lives and the people in their relational world. Reflection on theological beliefs and spirituality should not be thought of in binary categories (where spirituality is viewed as only life-giving or only life-limiting)—indeed, there might be constructive and destructive elements of both, such as is the case with morals and music as a form of spirituality as named above; there are grey areas in which religious scholars, psychotherapists, and community leaders need to discern how particular forms of spirituality functions in the lives of Black men.

In our reflection on key thinkers in Black religion and spirituality, Almeda Wright helps us think through the differences between fragmented spirituality and integrated spirituality. A Hope to Keep Going spirituality takes seriously the work of integrating all of life as a starting point for spirituality. Reflection on the Jeffries IV et al. article also helps us consider the ways that Black religious institutions have perpetuated heteronormativity in the lives of Black people. Nonetheless, despite Black religious institutions' non-tolerance of non-heterosexual norms, Black bisexual men in the Jeffries IV et al.'s study found a way to use spirituality as a resource when interpreted through the lens of their own life experiences as bisexual Black men, which helped them deal with condemnation they received from others on the basis of their sexual orientation. This finding points us to hope. That is, it demonstrates that by imagining, re-imagining, interpreting, and embodying spirituality through the lens of one's own life experiences, spirituality can serve as a resource to resist oppression, survive, and flourish in the world. Ultimately, spirituality in the lives of Black men is complex. Yet a Hope to Keep Going spirituality cultivates the survival, liberation, healing, and flourishing of Black men because it integrates all of life's experiences in the context of supportive community. The complex and nuanced experiences of Black men living in the United States and the larger world must be engaged in their fullness within the context of supportive community in order for spirituality to function as a life-giving, sustaining, and guiding resource for our lives. This is the aim of a Hope to Keep Going spirituality.

NOTES

1. This reflection emerged during a personal correspondence with Lee Butler Jr. in March 2018.

2. Watkins Jr., Tommie L., Cathy Simpson, Stacey S. Cofield, Susan Davies, Connie Kohler, and Stuart Usdan. "The Relationship of Religiosity, Spirituality, Substance Abuse, and Depression Among Black Men Who Have Sex with Men (MSM)," *Journal of Religion Health* 55, no. 1 (2016).

3. Namageyo-Funa et al., "The Role of Religion and Spirituality in Coping with Type 2 Diabetes: A Qualitative Study among Black Men," *Journal of Religion Health* (New York: Springer, 2015).

4. This is a reference to integrated spirituality as articulated by Almeda Wright. More will be said about integrated spirituality in subsequent pages of this chapter.

5. This is similar to the argument raised by thinkers such as Frantz Fanon.

6. We can also include the arts in general, such as visuals art, as examples of this form spirituality. While the men in this book did not explicitly name art forms outside of music as a form of spirituality, other art forms certainly bear characteristics of spirituality.

7. Almeda Wright, *The Spiritual Lives of Young African Americans* (New York: Oxford University Press, 2017), 1.

8. Wright, *The Spiritual Lives of Young African Americans,* 3.

9. Wright, *The Spiritual Lives of Young African Americans,* 3.

10. Wright, *The Spiritual Lives of Young African Americans*, 6.

11. Wright, *The Spiritual Lives of Young African Americans,* 6.

12. Wright, *The Spiritual Lives of Young African Americans*, 68.

13. Wright, *The Spiritual Lives of Young African Americans*, 85.

14. Wright, *The Spiritual Lives of Young African Americans*, 87.

15. William Jeffries IV, Brian Dodge, and Theo G. M. Sandfort, "Religion and Spirituality among Bisexual Black Men in the USA," *Culture, Health & Sexuality* 10, no. 5 (June, 2008), 463.

16. Jeffries IV, Dodge, and Sandfort, "Religion and Spirituality among Bisexual Black Men in the USA," 467.

17. Jeffries IV, Dodge, and Sandfort, "Religion and Spirituality among Bisexual Black Men in the USA," 468.

18. Jeffries IV, Dodge, and Sandfort, "Religion and Spirituality among Bisexual Black Men in the USA," 467.

19. Jeffries IV, Dodge, and Sandfort, "Religion and Spirituality among Bisexual Black Men in the USA," 472.

20. Wright, *The Spiritual Lives of Young African Americans*, 92.

21. Wright, *The Spiritual Lives of Young African Americans*, 114.

22. Wright, *The Spiritual Lives of Young African Americans*, 115.

23. While I reference Christianity and Islam here, it is important to acknowledge the presence of other expressions of Black spirituality, including Black Buddhists and Black Israelites, to name a few.

24. In many respects, terror continues to confront Black people in the United States and larger world.

25. Pinn, *Terror and Triumph: The Nature of Black Religion* (Minneapolis: Fortress Press, 2003), 81.

26. Pinn, *Terror and Triumph*, 81.

27. Pinn, *Terror and Triumph*, 83.

28. Pinn, *Terror and Triumph*, 83.

29. See Anne and Edward Wimberly's book, *Liberation and Human Wholeness*.

30. Pinn, *Terror and Triumph*, 90.

31. Pinn, *Terror and Triumph*, 99.

32. Pinn, *Terror and Triumph*, 109.

33. Pinn, *Terror and Triumph*, 130.

34. Pinn, *Terror and Triumph*, 141.

35. Pinn, *Terror and Triumph*, 157.

36. Pinn, *Terror and Triumph,* 157.

37. Pinn, *Terror and Triumph*, 158.

38. Pinn, *Terror and Triumph*, 158.

39. By purely psychological understandings I'm referring to psychological theories that split psychological experience from spiritual experience.

40. Pinn, *Terror and Triumph*, 159.

41. Jeffries IV, Dodge, and Sandfort, "Religion and Spirituality among Bisexual Black Men in the USA," 470.

42. Jeffries IV, Dodge, and Sandfort, "Religion and Spirituality among Bisexual Black Men in the USA," 470.

43. Jeffries IV, Dodge, and Sandfort, "Religion and Spirituality among Bisexual Black Men in the USA," 471.

Chapter Six

A Hope to Keep Going
Model of Change

Activating Communal Agency to Care for Black Men

The last chapter considered how an integrated Hope to Keep Going spirituality can contribute to the mental well-being of Black men. I argued that such a spirituality, drawing from West African roots, maintains a communal approach, integrates all of life's experiences, and remembers our ancestors while striving for a complex subjectivity.[1] This chapter is a continuation of that ethos and considers how community can participate in promoting the mental well-being of Black men. In *African American Psychology: From Africa to America*, the authors note that "when we speak of community, we are not simply talking about a geographic location, but a sense of social connection and belonging."[2] A sense of belonging is essential for Black men who are frequently alienated in society because of individual, institutional, and cultural racism in the United States and larger world. A Hope to Keep Going communal model of change is needed because there is a dearth of literature that takes seriously the complexities of Black men's social, intrapsychic, and spiritual experiences. This chapter takes seriously all of these complexities in a Black man's life in the context of community. Questions guiding the flow of this chapter are: What is happening in the social environments of Black men? What are the effects of the social environment in the lives of Black men? And, what is needed to change the environments in which Black men live so that they are more conducive for the survival, liberation, healing, and flourishing of Black men?

I have placed this chapter before the next chapter's exploration of an individual model of change because cultural and social contexts are more important as a starting point for discussion on the mental well-being of Black men than individual intrapsychic transformation. This is because intrapsychic experience is significantly affected by a person's cultural and social experiences in the world. Therefore, theories of the personality which do not take seriously the intricacies of the social environment fail to care optimally for the mental health of Black men. If we purify the polluted air that people breathe, we can reduce the number of people whose respiratory systems fail due to the polluted environment. Similarly, this chapter continues progress toward, metaphorically, purifying the air that Black men breathe so that Black men can have increased opportunities to survive and flourish in the world. A Hope to Keep Going communal model of change takes seriously the importance of understanding the nuances of the social contexts in which Black men live as important factors that should determine approaches to care and counseling with Black men. In this light, a Hope to Keep Going communal model of change acknowledges explicitly the contextual realities necessarily affecting the lives of Black men.

FACTORS ADDRESSED IN A HOPE TO KEEP GOING COMMUNAL MODEL OF CHANGE

The "hope" in a Hope to Keep Going model of change is found primarily in its *acknowledgment* of the issues affecting the lives of Black men that would otherwise prevent our survival, liberation, healing, and flourishing. This might seem like a simple task. Yet, the majority of theories of counseling and care ignore the relevant contextual facts affecting the lives of Black men. It is, therefore, critical to acknowledge explicitly factors impeding the survival and flourishing of Black men's mental well-being. Conversations with men in this book revealed obstacles that can impede the psychological and spiritual flourishing of Black men which must be addressed in a Hope to Keep Going communal model of change. The obstacles can be divided into the following six categories: *1) negative images and expectations of Black men in the media; 2) negative images and expectations of Black men in society; 3) negative treatment of Black men in society; 4) [some] Black men lacking empathy and support for the experiences and ambitions of women; 5) appreciating women primarily for the pleasure women bring to men;* and *6) [some] Black men embodying a moral ethic that dehumanizes LGBTQIA people.* A Hope to Keep Going communal model of change addresses all these factors negatively affecting the identities and experiences of Black men. These factors limit Black men's ability to survive and flourish in the world. By naming these six obstacles, we affirm that they are part of the *social pathology* negatively affecting the lives of Black men. Addressing these aspects of social pathology makes it possible to develop constructive images of Black male identity which are life-giving for Black men and the people in relationship with Black men. That is, a Hope to Keep Going communal model of change is focused on seeing social pathology and working to "cure" it so that Black men have increased opportunities to survive and flourish in the world.

Regarding the first obstacle, *negative images and expectations of Black men in the media*, the men in this book affirmed that the media influences people's perceptions of Black men. As Gregory C. Ellison, II noted, this is not just a value neutral gaze, but is a *punitive* gaze.[3] African American men are viewed as criminals and "the worst of the worst."[4] According to Black men in this book, the media and society believes Black men are *dumb, not educated, criminals, violent, a threat, evil, thugs, and savages*. Concerning the second obstacle, *negative images and expectations of Black men in society*, the men in this book shared that society has expectations for the ultimate life destinations of Black men, which include: incarceration, being killed by the police, or becoming successful as a professional entertainer. The third obstacle, *negative treatment of Black men in society,* names that Black men in this book revealed that they are not known by the people they encounter in the world, particularly by non-Black people. As a result, they are treated in ways that are guided by the negative images and expectations that the media and dominant culture maintains of Black men. The men in this book communicated that they are "Strongly . . . looked at [by] the police . . . [and] other people, like we're monsters" and "look[ed] at like we're so scary as a black man." In this sense, Black men are hyper-visible in American society. Amidst these hyper-visible realities, they expressed a desire for peace. Existing as objects, or "monsters" as named by Jamal, in U.S. society, men in this book expressed that they are treated as if their lives have less value than police dogs, police officers, and other non-Black people. All these factors contribute to a lack of peace in moments of their lives. In addition to being treated as if they have less value than other people in society, they expressed that they have been questioned and excluded from groups and, in this regard, alienated from society's rich well of resources. Finally, they revealed that they are expected "to act a certain way," meaning that if a Black man is *educated, intelligent, not a criminal, not violent, not a threat,* and *not a thug or savage,* then he is "not your average black guy."[5] Living amidst these negative images, expectations, and treatment of Black men in U.S. society poses significant stressors and obstacles for the psychological well-being of Black men. The fourth obstacle names that *[some] Black men lack empathy and support for the experiences and ambitions of women.* Men in this book identified themselves as providers and protectors of women. Yet, they functioned as providers and protectors without having empathy and extending support for the experiences and ambitions of women. Similarly, the fifth obstacle is that men in this book *appreciated women primarily for the pleas-*

ure women bring to men. The sixth obstacle highlights that *[some] Black men embody a moral ethic that dehumanizes LGBTQIA people.* A Hope to Keep Going theory of communal change resists any Black male identity that does not support the survival, liberation, healing, and flourishing of women and LGBTQIA people. Therefore, all the obstacles listed above must be resisted in a Hope to Keep Going communal model of change. A Hope to Keep Going communal model of change aims to support, develop, and cultivate conscious[6] Black men who can survive and flourish amidst the vast array of obstacles impeding the survival and flourishing of Black men. A conscious Black man is one who is aware of the realities of racism, sexism, heterosexism, homophobia, and classism (including their historical, contemporary, systemic, and institutional underpinnings and manifestations). Certainly this can include awareness of other forms of oppression. For the purposes of this book, racism, sexism, heterosexism, homophobia, and classism are highlighted as forms of oppression that impede the survival, liberation, healing, and flourishing of Black men.

PERSPECTIVES OF KEY THINKERS ON FACTORS IMPEDING THE FLOURISHING OF BLACK MEN

Political Solidarity Against Anti-Black Racism

Key thinkers who have reflected on the realities of race and racism can aid our efforts to care for the mental well-being of Black men. African and African American Studies and Philosophy professor Tommie Shelby proposes a Black political solidarity aimed at the liberation of Black people in such a way that gives Black people the right to choose our own identity. Shelby's position is helpful for our model of communal change because he emphasizes the value of individuals and groups working together to resist antiblack racism. A Hope to Keep Going communal model of change, therefore, takes seriously the importance of groups and communities collectively working together to resist and dismantle antiblack racism and the negative ways that antiblack racism affects Black men.

Shelby's work aims to liberate Black people from the injustices which stem from antiblack racism and presents a Black politics, which addresses the ways that Black people can work together to reduce the burden of antiblack racism on our lives. For Shelby, we can reduce the burden of antiblack racism by engaging in the work of Black solidarity using the philosophy of Black pragmatic nationalism. A Hope to Keep Going communal model of change affirms and adopts Shelby's philosophy of Black pragmatic nationalism as a foundational philosophical tenet guiding our approach to the care of Black men. Black solidarity, from the vantage point of Black pragmatic nationalism, is "committed to defeating racism, to eliminating unjust racial inequalities, and to improve the material life prospects of those racialized as 'black,' especially the most disadvantaged."[7] According to Shelby, there should be a "commitment to antiracism, antipoverty, and substantive racial equality."[8] For Black people, it is this commitment to antiracism, antipoverty, and substantive racial equality that should determine one's Blackness.

In order to cultivate a political solidarity committed to defeating antiblack racism, Shelby identifies the "need to rethink the foundations of African American solidarity" and to "reevaluate the very idea of black political unity."[9] According to Shelby, the focus of Black solidarity must shift from *social identity* to *racial injustice*. He acknowledges that many political philosophers hold that Black people must retain their racial identity to achieve "political solidarity, cultural identity, and group self-realization."[10] Yet, this is in opposition to Shelby's notion of Black pragmatic nationalism because his approach does not consider adopting a particular form of cultural Blackness as a central component of political solidarity.

He explicitly opposes Black cultural nationalism in favor of a pragmatic nationalist view which asserts that Blacks can come together on the basis of fighting a commonly experienced oppression of antiblack racism. He notes that Du Bois was concerned with a collective Black identity that was "based primarily on a shared history and culture, and only secondarily on a common biological inheritance," and that Du Bois believed this collective identity was necessary for an emancipatory black solidarity.[11] However, Shelby emphasizes that an emancipatory Black political solidarity must be separated from a collective Black identity and calls for an abandonment of the types of Black unity and political thought that stresses the need for "racial, ethnic, cultural, and national identity."[12]

Much like Victor Anderson, Shelby acknowledges difference among Black people. Portraying positive and diverse images of Black men in the media and society is critical for the mental well-being of Black men. Shelby is concerned with liberating Black people by opening up possibilities for Blacks to have the freedom to choose our identity without being forced to fit into a particular understand of cultural Blackness. He notes that not everybody who is Black self-identifies with particular forms of cultural blackness. For Shelby, such individuals should not be condemned for their choice of cultural identification which may deviate from an accepted norm as dictated by Black Nationalism. From this perspective, it is important for Blacks to have the right to cultural autonomy. Maintaining a position of decentralizing culture as an essential component of Black Nationalism, Shelby holds that it is possible for Blacks to fight against White cultural imperialism without giving in to a collective cultural consciousness.[13]

Shelby's discourse on the concepts of thin blackness and thick blackness is particularly helpful for understanding his position on Black identity. He notes that the concept of thin Blackness identifies persons as Black if they: 1) have the biological traits; and 2) if they are descendants of sub-Saharan Africa. These people have no choice but to identify racially as Black. On the other hand, thick Blackness has additional requirements. He identifies five modes of thick Blackness as: 1) *Racialist*—"based on the supposed presence of a special genotype in the biological makeup of all (fully) black people that does not exist among nonblacks"[14]; 2) *Ethnic*—based on a common ancestral heritage; 3) *Nationality*—based on one's affiliation and commitment to a particular nation; 4) *Cultural*—based on the claim that there are certain held "beliefs, values, conventions, traditions, and practices that is distinctively black"; and 5) *kinship*.[15] Shelby argues that the thin concept of Blackness may be helpful for Black political solidarity, yet the thick concept of Blackness does not offer Blacks the autonomy to freely choose their identity. While Shelby acknowledges that theorists of collective identity theory support the idea of thick Blackness, he notes that a person cannot choose whether or not she is thinly black, but she can determine how she will live out her thin Blackness. According to Shelby's concept of black pragmatic nationalism, all people should have an obligation to participate in acts of resistance towards racial injustice.[16]

Additionally, Shelby's description of authenticity is helpful for a Hope to Keep Going communal model of change because it helps us consider constructive and life-affirming definitions of "authentic" Blackness. Shelby suggests that we can use the term "inauthenticity" to refer to one who is not faithful to her or his commitments to black solidarity. In opposition to inauthenticity, "authenticity" consists of "being faithful to the practical principles that one has freely adopted."[17] Authentic Black people *freely* choose our "practical principles" and faithfully live up to our commitments to political solidarity.

Pragmatically, Shelby asserts that Blacks should 1) "maintain their political solidarity with each other 2) and cultivate greater bonds of unity with progressive members of other racial groups."[18] The goal of Shelby's position and method is to move toward a racially just society. To achieve a racially just society, Blacks must move from a collective identity which is ethnocultural to one which is political.[19] His approach of pragmatic black nationalism "aims simply to remove the obstacles to individual autonomy caused by racial injustice."[20] Such an approach guides the ethos of a Hope to Keep Going communal model of change.

Hearing Our Story, Acknowledging Our Presence

Having explored Shelby's pragmatic black nationalism, we now explore African American professor and critical race theorist Patricia Williams' work as we consider the philosophical underpinnings of a Hope to Keep Going communal model of change. Williams begins her book, *The Alchemy of Race and Rights,* with a historical account illustrating how Blacks who were en-slaved and tried to run away from slavery were considered stupid or crazy. This account illustrates that even though Blacks were simply trying to attain freedom, they were characterized by their White slave masters as crazy, ignorant, and subservient. By offering this historical perspective, Williams helps us see that a worldview which affirms Blacks as crazy, inferior, and subservient to Whites has strong historical roots dating back to slavery. While chattel slavery no longer exists, it is wise for those caring for the mental health of Black men to consider the ways that oppressive power dynamics might be present in contemporary society so that Black men and allies can resist oppressive power dynamics that would otherwise character-ize Black men as crazy, inferior, and subservient beings simply for their pursuit of freedom from injustice.

Much like Angela Harris and Emma Jordan's argument of unmasking biases masked in false claims of neutrality and objectivity, Williams chal-lenges the "objective truths" of Western society that don't allow for differ-ence, which, in turn, paralyzes any attempt at justice. She notes that Western society has long existed without examining these objective truths and has not acknowledged their subjective nature. There is, hence, a dynamic in which racism, claiming objective truths, has projected criminality as well as other forms of evil onto Black people.[21] The danger of such a projection is that Black people in America are vulnerable to projective identification that has the ability to cause Black people to identify with the negative projections that White-supremacist ideology places onto Black people. Williams notes that racism imposes itself onto the psyches of Black people in such a way that keeps the self from fully seeing itself.[22] A Hope to Keep Going commu-nal model change, therefore, takes seriously the need for communities to see Black people free from the constraints of White-supremacist and White-normative lenses.

Positive Contributions to Society

Williams also contends that a racist worldview prevents people from accept-ing any valuable contribution to society by a Black person. To illustrate this point, she tells the story of a person named Fred—a descendant of German Jews and schooled in England—who was disturbed by the idea that the musician and composer Beethoven was "black" or mulatto. However, once Fred conducted his own research and discovered that this was in fact true, his perception of Beethoven changed; all of a sudden, he heard the music of Beethoven differently.[23] He no longer viewed the music of Beethoven with a sense of awe (as was his original take on the famous musician when he believed that Beethoven was White without any trace of "black" or mulatto). Williams shared this story to illustrate that Black people are not afforded the freedom to claim our contributions to the world.[24] Rather, the contributions of Black people are viewed as a threat to Western society. Yet, she declares that the greatest threat to Western civilization will be the realization that Black people have contributed and been a part of Western civilization all along.[25] A Hope to Keep Going communal model of change explicitly acknowledges, welcomes, and nurtures non-hegemonic contributions to society by Black men so that Black men are equally valued participants in society.

Emmanuel Lartey's Model of Social Therapy

While Shelby and Williams provide theoretical perspectives that ground a Hope to Keep Going communal model of change, Emmanuel Lartey's model of social therapy can help us reflect further on what a communal model of change might look like in practice. Emmanuel Lartey presents a model of social therapy, in his book *In Living Color: An Intercultural Approach to Pastoral Care and Counseling*, that is helpful for guiding diverse groups to work together toward therapeutic and liberating change in communities. The model is guided by the disciplines of pastoral care and counseling and liberation theology. Lartey's model for social therapy is cyclical and includes the following points: A) *Recognition* (self-awareness); B) *Identification* (of people and issues); C) *Befriending* (knowing and being known); D) *Working Together in Groups*; and E) *Acting Together* (symbolically, socially, and politically).[26] A Hope to Keep Going communal model of change affirms and adopts Lartey's model of social therapy with one additional concept. A Hope to Keep Going communal model of change adds the concept of "be-familying" to Lartey's model of social therapy, instead of "be-friending." The term "be-familying" is offered here because of the implications and importance of viewing another person as part of one's family, particularly when working with diverse groups of people who might not ordinarily view the other as family. Patricia Williams provides a good example to further illustrate this point. In Williams' book *The Alchemy of Race and Rights*, she tells a story of a White manager who believed the narrative of a White usher who beat a Black teenager in the alley of a movie theater. Not only did the White manager not believe the Black teenager; the manager also did not believe the older Black adults who tried to convince the White manager that the Black teenager was beaten by the White usher. Rather, the White manager sided with the White usher who expressed that the Black teenager was the cause of trouble. The White usher was never punished. Williams tells this story to illustrate that if the Black-older-adult advocates could not be believed, then her chances of being believed (as a young person at the time of the story) would be minimal. She questioned what this incident at the movie theater meant for her place and voice in the world. Would she be believed? Because the White usher was considered family by the White manager (and therefore extended empathy and support from the White manager), the Blacks and others, who were advocating for the Black boy who was beaten in the alley, were not believed. In other words, if you are not family, you cannot be believed. In this story, a White person did not view Blacks and the other non-Whites in the movie theater as family. If Black men are to survive and thrive in the world, communities must work together so that Black men are viewed as members of the human family.

HOPE TO KEEP GOING COMMUNAL AGENCY

In order for a communal model of change to significantly and positively affect the lives of Black men, communities must embody, develop, and maintain empathy for the emotional experiences of Black men. Caring for the emotional experiences of Black men must no longer be considered as an afterthought in our pursuits of justice. Embodying empathy takes time and intentionality. In this vein, communal agency from the purview of a Hope to Keep Going communal model of change means that communities must collectively *reflect, develop and maintain awareness, support,* and *engage in social justice activism* to nurture the survival, liberation, healing, and flourishing of Black men. The activation of communal agency is significant, as evident in the life-giving ways that Black communities have historically benefited from the power of collective action (highlighting the importance of Ubunto: "I am because we are") and because of an intersubjective view of reality which affirms that we mutually influence one another and are, in turn, affected by the actions of others. The community must rally behind critical issues of social injustice so that the psyches of Black men are not overloaded with heavy emotional and spiritual burdens just to survive in the world.

Let's consider the tenets of communal agency as defined by a Hope to Keep Going communal model of change. It is critical for the community to adopt a mode of being in which it continually *reflects* on the negative images, expectations, and treatment affecting Black men and the overall current state of Black people in the United States and larger world. Reflection, in this sense, is concerned with questions such as: 1) How are we as a community? 2) What's happening in our world? and 3) Where are we in the history of our collective journey toward justice, liberation, and flourishing as a human race? *Developing and maintaining awareness* means that a community gains adequate awareness of specific issues, and, for our purposes, the specific negative images, expectations, and treatment of Black men. As the community maintains awareness, it must *support* Black men on the critical aforementioned issues which pose a threat to the human flourishing of Black men. Amidst cultural environments where Black men are chronically disregarded, disrespected, discredited, feared, and devalued, fostering spaces and relation-

ships for Black men to feel understood is critical in the process of nurturing
Black men's flourishing. The community possesses the power to serve as
life-affirming selfobjects in the lives of Black men. An aspect of support
includes providing places of refuge for Black men. Places of refuge should
be developed and maintained by Black people for Black men. Yet, in addition, and following the lead of Derrick Bell, within the context of the United
States, Black people may also need well-meaning White people to advocate
for the survival, liberation, healing, and flourishing of Black men and provide places of refuge. As Bell notes, "black people may need places of refuge
and whites to provide escape from future betrayals."[27] While supporting the
emotional lives of Black men through developing and maintaining empathic
attunement with Black men's intrapsychic experiences, the community must
also act to counter the negative images and expectations of Black men so that
social environments will become less toxic and more conducive for the survival and flourishing of Black men. This is done through *social justice activism.* The idea embraced here is that we must fight for justice with all we
got! Communities advocating for the mental well-being of Black men
should, in the spirit of Derrick Bell and the group N.W.A., "express yo'self!"
An element of expression is resisting the oppressive norms of racism, sexism, classism, heteronormativity, and other oppressive cultural, systemic,
and institutional evils, which limit opportunities for the survival and flourishing of Black men. Social justice activism is a form of communal agency
which helps Black men obtain material and educational resources necessary
for living a meaningful life and surviving and thriving in the world.

HOPE TO KEEP GOING
COMMUNAL MODEL OF CHANGE

Figure 6.1 illustrates the Hope to Keep Going communal cycle of change
offered in this book. A premise of the cycle is that Black communities *and*
Black men must engage in this process of change to survive and, ultimately,
flourish in the world. In other words, Black communities who care for Black
men can use this cycle as a guide for their formation and development process as they seek to care for the mental health of Black men. Likewise, the
cycle is created so that communities can nurture in individual Black men the
emotional tools necessary to live into each of the phases of the cycle as
necessary throughout their lifetime. The cycle assumes that Black communities and Black men must first survive before healing, liberation, and flourishing are possible. Following survival, the ability to resist oppressive ideologies, cultures, institutions, and relationships is critical at every phase in a
Black community's and Black man's life. Resistance is critical for Black
men because of the chronic nature in which they feel disregarded, disre-

Figure 6.1.   A Hope to Keep Going Communal Cycle of Change Diagram by Nicholas Grier

spected, discredited, feared, and devalued. Black men experience these forms of oppression because of the presence of racism, classism, heterosexism, and other forms of oppression in society which dehumanize Black men's very existence. Black men must also resist sexist, machoistic, and homophobic notions of Black masculinity as these forms of oppression compromise Black male identity and harm Black men's relationships with women and other Black men. After resisting all forms of oppression in a Black community's and Black man's life, emotional healing must take place quickly so that Black communities and Black men are ready for the next inevitable bullet of oppression (a figurative and, in other moments, literal bullet). Once Black communities and Black men survive, resist, and experience healing, liberation can occur. Liberation is the state in which Black communities and Black men are free from the constraints of mental, material, and physical bondage. Yet, even after liberation occurs, resistance must recur, and healing must be reinforced. Only after survival, resistance, healing, and liberation have occurred is flourishing possible. Flourishing is the state in which Black communities and Black men live fully into liberated identities. It is not simply being free from the oppression (as is the case for the liberation phase of the cycle); rather, flourishing is the state of fully actualizing ourselves in ways that are life-giving to ourselves and others. Flourishing is the state of living fully into all the tenets of human flourishing outlined in the introduction of this book. Flourishing is necessarily a decolonial activity. Because of the inevitable nature of oppression in the world in which Black communities and Black men live, Black communities and Black men must continually resist oppression, even after having attained flourishing. Because of the emotional energy that Black communities and Black men exert continually resisting oppression, Black communities and Black men must engage continually in the process of emotional and spiritual healing. After healing occurs, Black communities and Black men can return to flourishing. By continuously resisting oppression and engaging in the process of healing, Black communities and Black men are positioned to survive and flourish in the world.

I have also inserted the "Constantly Becoming Woke" circle in the middle of figure 6.1. This circle is placed in the middle of the diagram to illustrate that Black communities and Black men must grow continually in our awareness of systems of oppression and the ways that we operate in the world. By constantly becoming woke, Black communities and Black men can maintain a grounded center to return, which nurtures continuously renewed life-giving visions of our collective and individual selves. Communal approaches to the care of Black men must nurture each of the phases identified in the Hope to Keep Going communal cycle of change.

Additionally, another premise of the Hope to Keep Going cycle of change is that Black communities and Black men must celebrate the joys of life and maintain a spirit of gratitude throughout their lifetime. Celebration acknowledges the triumphs and beauty of life and helps communities and Black men maintain a spirit of joy. Dancing, singing, playing music, creating visual art, and spending time with friends are examples of ways that Black communities and Black men have celebrated the joys of life. While these are examples of celebratory practices, Black communities and Black men should celebrate in whatever ways are life-giving to them if celebratory practices are to contribute to their survival, healing, liberation, and flourishing. A Hope to Keep Going communal cycle of change holds that Black communities and Black men should celebrate throughout their lifetime and imagine and re-imagine their celebratory practices so that they experience fully the joys of life. Similarly, embodying a spirit of gratitude helps Black communities and Black men recall and give thanks for all of life's blessings. Celebrating and maintaining a spirit of gratitude, in this sense, does not condone systems of oppression. Rather, celebrating and giving thanks throughout life positions Black communities and Black men to discover and experience fully the joys of life free from the constraints of oppressive cultures, systems, and institutions.

Lastly, in order to support the well-being of Black men, communities must also explore, identify, present, and make possible a variety of ways for a person to be both Black and male. As the colloquial saying goes: "We are not all the same." Eddie expressed this sentiment during our first conversation:

> you have the image of I would guess you say the thug that's perpetuated by the media and a lot of different instances from TV to movies to even the news plays a large factor on how they portraying black males. So most the images you see in the media of black men is either they're going to jail or they're being killed by police. If you look at the imagery in the media now, you don't see too many intellectuals, and then if you see somebody that's an intellectual, . . . they don't show the knowledgeable conscious black male in the media. They'll show more of the Uncle Tom or the Sambo in the media.

In the spirit of Eddie's observations, a Hope to Keep Going communal cycle of change advocates for the establishment, development, and maintenance of spaces where Black men can process life critically and imagine a variety of ways to creatively and constructively be both Black and male.

A Hope to Keep Going communal model of change advocates for the total well-being of Black men. It does so by encouraging communities to participate in all of the following tasks which maintain as their focus the survival, liberation, healing, and flourishing of Black men: 1) Connecting Black men with a guide and/or counselor;[28] 2) Connecting Black men with supportive groups to constructively process life experiences. If such groups do not exist in one's local area, those caring for Black men should work to create and develop such groups; 3) Creating and developing social environments that promote the survival, liberation, healing, and flourishing of Black men. A part of this task includes resisting injustice at the city, state, and federal level. Social justice advocacy and organizing for Black men fall within this category; 4) Creating and developing institutional cultures (such as schools and places of employment) conducive for the survival, liberation, healing, and flourishing of Black men; and 5) Creating and developing the arts and media in ways that promote the survival, liberation, healing, and flourishing of Black men. When leaders, communities, mental health professionals, and all those who care about Black men, work together to accomplish these five tasks, Black men have increased opportunities to survive and flourish. One role of a mental health professional working with Black men, therefore, is to point Black men to opportunities to participate in community in ways outlined above. Likewise, a mental health professional concerned with the mental well-being of Black men will work to participate in one or more of these tasks. Only after we have explored fully the community's role in nurturing the mental well-being of Black men[29] should we consider the individual (intrapsychic) experiences of Black men. After having fully explored the community's role in the care of Black men, we can turn our attention to caring for Black men's individual emotional experiences, which is the task of the next chapter.

NOTES

1. This book's conception of complex subjectivity derives from the work of Anthony B. Pinn as outlined in the previous chapter.

2. Faye Z. Belgrave and Kevin W. Allison, *African American Psychology: From Africa to America* (Thousand Oaks: Sage Publications, 2019), 195.

3. Professional correspondence in December 2016.

4. As articulated by research participant, Darrell.

5. As expressed by research participant, Kendrick.

6. In this sentence, I am using the phrase "conscious Black men" as a term to identify Black men who are aware of the ways that oppression operates in society.

7. Tommie Shelby, *We Who Are Dark: The Philosophical Foundations of Black Solidarity* (Cambridge: The Belknap Press of Harvard University Press, 2005), 4.

8. Shelby, *We Who Are Dark: The Philosophical Foundations of Black Solidarity*, 161.

9. Shelby, *We Who Are Dark: The Philosophical Foundations of Black Solidarity*, 2.

10. Shelby, *We Who Are Dark: The Philosophical Foundations of Black Solidarity*, 3.

11. Shelby, *We Who Are Dark: The Philosophical Foundations of Black Solidarity*, 206.

12. Shelby, *We Who Are Dark: The Philosophical Foundations of Black Solidarity*, 206.

13. Shelby, *We Who Are Dark: The Philosophical Foundations of Black Solidarity*, 169.

14. Shelby, *We Who Are Dark: The Philosophical Foundations of Black Solidarity*, 209.

15. Shelby, *We Who Are Dark: The Philosophical Foundations of Black Solidarity*, 211.

16. Shelby, *We Who Are Dark: The Philosophical Foundations of Black Solidarity*, 214.

17. Shelby, *We Who Are Dark: The Philosophical Foundations of Black Solidarity*, 215.

18. Shelby, *We Who Are Dark: The Philosophical Foundations of Black Solidarity*, 242.

19. Shelby, *We Who Are Dark: The Philosophical Foundations of Black Solidarity*, 244.

20. Shelby, *We Who Are Dark: The Philosophical Foundations of Black Solidarity*, 252.

21. Patricia Williams, *The Alchemy of Race and Rights: Diary of a Law Professor* (Cambridge: Harvard University Press, 1991), 61.

22. Williams, *The Alchemy of Race and Rights: Diary of a Law Professor*, p. 63

23. Williams, *The Alchemy of Race and Rights: Diary of a Law Professor*, 12.

24. Williams, *The Alchemy of Race and Rights: Diary of a Law Professor*, 114.

25. Williams, *The Alchemy of Race and Rights: Diary of a Law Professor*, 115.

26. Emmanuel Y. Lartey, *In Living Color: An Intercultural Approach to Pastoral Care and Counseling*, 2nd edition (London: Jessica Kingsley Publishers, 2003), 134.

27. Bell, *Faces at the Bottom of the Well: The Permanence of Racisim* (New York: Basic Books, 1992), 108.

28. The guide and/or counselor must also be aware of the pertinent issues facing Black male life in order to best serve as a guide and/or counselor who can help spark the survival, liberation, healing and flourishing of Black men.

29. The tasks of considering the community's role in cultivating the mental well-being of Black men is not a one-time occurrence. Rather, those caring for Black men should continually reflect on the community's role in cultivating the mental well-being of Black men.

Chapter Seven

A Hope to Keep Going Model of Change

Activating Creative and Constructive Agency in Black Men

Having named essential components of a Hope to Keep Going communal model of change in the previous chapter, this chapter offers a method for interpreting and caring for the intrapsychic experiences of Black men to improve therapeutic responses to Black men. There is currently very little written on the intrapsychic experiences of Black men within the disciplines of spiritual care, counseling, and psychology. I am, therefore, appropriating the voices of Black men in this book into theory to give sufficient account and description of their intrapsychic experiences while considering the challenges and opportunities for their survival, liberation, healing, and flourishing. The discussion in this chapter aims to offer a way to understand the psychological experiences of Black men so that spiritual caregivers, mental health professionals, and community leaders can more adequately care for the lives of Black men.

This chapter's model of change draws from Phillis Sheppard's critical appropriation of self psychology, Lee Butler's Theory of African American Communal Identity Formation, critical race theorists, and the stories of Black men to equip religious leaders, mental health professionals, community leaders, and all people, with a resource to care optimally for the mental well-being of Black men. While a premise of a Hope to Keep Going framework for care and counseling affirms, as a starting point, the importance of communities caring for the social environments and cultures in which Black men live, communities can also be othering and fall short of affirming fully the unique experiences of individual Black men. It is because of this reality that a Hope to Keep Going framework for care and counseling must tend to the intrapsychic experiences of Black men. In other words, the unique individual life experiences of a Black man can be lost in the spirit of community if we do not care for the depth intrapsychic experiences of individual Black men. This is not an argument for individualism. Rather, it is an affirmation of caring for the particular emotional experiences and material realities of individual Black men with the expectation that those caring for Black men will encourage them to live in life-giving and supportive community.

THE IMPACT OF CULTURAL SELFOBJECTS ON THE INTRAPSYCHIC EXPERIENCES OF BLACK MEN

As a way to engage the intrapsychic experiences of Black men, I refer to Heinz Kohut, who developed the theory of self psychology. Kohut considered the state of the self as critical for psychological well-being. According to Kohut's bipolar nature of the self, an individual has *mirroring* and *idealizing* needs. Kohut would later develop *twinship* as a third need of the self, which developed out of his concept of mirroring. The needs of the self are met by selfobjects.[1] According to Kohut, we never get over these three needs of the self: mirroring selfobjects, idealizing selfobjects, and twinship selfobjects. *Mirroring* refers to an individual's need to be known and to have one's experiences and ambitions acknowledged by others. *Idealizing* refers to a person's need to believe in something greater than one's self. Finally, *twinship* refers to a need to be with one who is somewhat like one's self. The theory of self psychology maintains that the cohesive self achieves maturity when an individual can navigate through life with healthy mirroring, idealizing, and twinship selfobjects.

I also find Kohut's theory of change helpful for the process of nurturing the survival, liberation, healing, and flourishing of Black men. Central to his theory of change, Kohut's notion of *transmuting internalization* occurs when healthy selfobjects are internalized and function as a resource for a cohesive nuclear self. Critical to the therapeutic process and to the laying down of new psychological structure is the need for the therapist (or, for our purposes, community leaders, the community, and culture) to display empathic attunement. A Hope to Keep Going model of change affirms that individual therapists and the community must be empathically attuned with the experiences of Black men. Kohut defines empathy as a two-step process of *understanding* and *explanation.* For the purposes of understanding the intrapsychic experiences of Black men, consideration is given here to understanding the complexity of family, communal, and cultural selfobjects and to discovering how they impact the intrapsychic experiences of Black men.

While Kohut made an important contribution to understanding psychological life by placing emphasis on an individual's need for selfobjects throughout one's lifetime, and naming the importance of empathy in the therapeutic process, the claim here is that Kohut's theory is not sufficient on its own to understand the psychological experiences and needs of Black men. Rather, a critical appropriation of self psychology, such as one offered by Phillis Sheppard, is necessary for the theory to provide a helpful framework for understanding the intrapsychic experiences of Black men.

Sheppard provides a womanist framework of self psychology and views the "self [as] simultaneously a cultural and psychic experience."[2] She further notes that "to theorize the self involves theorizing the relational and the contextual."[3] Sheppard helps us understand the importance of cultural selfobjects from a womanist perspective. She notes that "[w]omanist thought as appropriated by pastoral theologians aims to name the cultural dislocation of black experience and black modes of social and personal transformation and healing."[4] Additionally, womanist pastoral theology is "not primarily individual but [also] contextual and communal."[5] Womanist pastoral theology's commitment to individuals, context, and communal care, while taking seriously the particular experiences of Black women, leads me to integrate Sheppard's womanist thought in our discussion on the care of Black men.

BLACK MEN'S POSITIVE CULTURAL SELFOBJECTS

While Black men face many challenges to possessing positive selfobjects as resources for human flourishing, it is nonetheless vitally important to acknowledge the positive selfobjects present in the psyches of Black men and to refrain from approaching the care of Black men with the lens of a deficit psychological perspective. There are positive selfobjects in the psyches of Black men that must be acknowledged and fortified.[6] Here, I am thinking of the constructive role and function of spaces such as Black barbershops, which often foster opportunities for constructive reflection, discussion, and relationship-building centered on promoting the emotional, relational, spiritual, and material well-being of Black men. The genuine support of the barbershop owner in this book who opened his barbershop for the focus group is evidence of this reality. To fortify communal support for Black men, the presence of people like the barbershop owner in this book must continue and be considered as an essential resource to aid the mental well-being of Black men. Similarly, the men in this book benefited from positive relationships with their mothers, uncles, and grandmothers. In this sense, empathic attunement with the needs of young Black men through life-giving community and family relationships must continue and improve in order to cultivate the future survival, liberation, healing, and flourishing of Black men.

UNDERSTANDING THE
INTRAPSYCHIC EXPERIENCES OF BLACK MEN

While there are positive selfobjects in the lives of Black men, there are negative selfobjects in the cultural milieu—because of racism, sexism, heterosexism, homophobia, and classism—that deeply affect the intrapsychic experiences of Black men. It is important to gain an understanding of common internal emotions, and their origins, of Black men. As highlighted in previous chapters, the psyches of Black men in this book are very active. Amidst their active minds, and the accompanying stressors of living in social environments that are committed to the workings of racism, sexism, classism, and heteronormativity, Black men yearn to be understood. Yet, Black men in this book embodied, and in certain moments, explicitly communicated, a belief that nobody cares about their lives. Amidst this psychosocial reality, spiritual caregivers, mental health professionals, and community leaders can make a positive difference in the lives of Black men by taking the time to listen deeply and care for their intrapsychic experiences. A critical dimension of care, in this regard, includes providing empathy and resources for Black men in the early stages of life when Black males are infants and children. Through relational experiences with early-life caregivers and parental figures, along with experiences with culture, Black men can gain the psychological and spiritual tools necessary to survive and flourish in the world.

Spiritual caregivers, counselors, and community leaders must also acknowledge Black men's common internal emotions of hurt, woundedness, and sadness, which are often masked in Black men's expressions of anger and frustration. Treated unfairly on an ongoing basis, Black men in this book communicated that they can only be frustrated for so long. Specifically, Jamal named his mental process as follows: 1) initial anger about the social injustices, which negatively impact his life; 2) desire to fight; 3) thinking through the consequences of his actions (if he were to fight); and 4) adjusting his mindset to consider the potential negative consequences of his actions. The fact that he wanted to fight in the first place demonstrates that he was not happy with the way he was treated. We can observe that in such a state, the feeling of peace is absent. Amidst the turmoil of living life as chronically disregarded, disrespected, discredited, feared, and devalued, Black men in this book demonstrated that they yearn for peace. Central, therefore, to the care of Black men is the need to help Black men have a sense of peace amidst daily negative treatment. This is not a peace that is complicit with oppression. Rather, it is a type of peace that enables a Black man to be human and make it to the next moment with clarity of thought and resolve to keep going toward a better future.

One of the ways that the psyches of Black men in this book were active is in exerting mental energy imaging the mindsets of White people. They thought about how White people look at them as Black men (e.g., as criminals and people who will snatch a woman's purse). They have also viewed Whites as people who steal from Black people for their own economic and personal gains. Further, the men in this book acknowledged that White people have the power to "fire me quick." Any theory and practice of care and counseling with Black men must acknowledge the intrapsychic implications of these realities affecting their psyches.

Black men in this book demonstrated that another aspect of exerting energy imagining the mindsets of White people is comparing the treatment of Black people to the treatment of White people. According to men in this book, Black people are not granted the same privileges as White people. One example of privilege is that White people are deemed credible and accepted upon first sight while Black men are often disregarded, disrespected, discredited, feared, and devalued upon first sight.

Amidst being viewed through a negative and often punitive lens, the men in this book exhibited an ability to psychologically resist the negative cultural images and expectations of Black men present in the media and society. It is, therefore, important to acknowledge that psychological resistance is an important dimension of psychological survival, liberation, healing, and flourishing in the lives of Black men. Psychological resistance enabled the men in this book to have opportunities to survive and flourish against all odds. As an act of resistance, one of the ways that they resisted was to turn away from negativity in order to avoid falling victim to a downwards psychological spiral which would, in turn, negatively affect: 1) Black men's outlook on life; and 2) Black men's relationships with other people. Therefore, to avoid these negative consequences, they made choices to turn their attention away from negativity about Black men. A second way of resisting was proving the negative images and expectations of Black men in the media and society wrong by living in such a way that counters these images and expectations. While this second way of resisting provides opportunities for embodying and displaying life-affirming images of Black masculinity, it is wise to consider *the psychological effects of always having to work harder to prove the negative images and expectations of Black men in the media and society wrong.* An accurate understanding of the psyches of Black men must give adequate attention to the energy dispensed countering negative images and expectations of Black men in society. Additionally, the claim here is that it is necessary to resist and prove wrong the negative images and expectations of Black men. This is because the power of projection and introjection have damaging effects on the psyches of Black men when that which is projected onto Black men is life-limiting. In this regard, Black men must be free of the burden of negative images and expectations of Black men projected onto them by the

media and society. While the prevalence of racism makes it extremely difficult for Black men to live in a world where there are no negative projections
on the lives of Black men, it is possible to reduce the number of negative
projections on Black men through the collective efforts of individual Black
men and communities who act with an intention to dismantle the negative
cultural images and expectations of Black men in the media and society.
Activism and community organizing for the sake of justice will also aid these
efforts. To care optimally for the psyches of Black men, those caring for
Black men must be empathically attuned with the psychological needs of
Black men as they work hard to prove the negative images and expectations
of themselves wrong. The psyches of Black men are at risk for psychological
exhaustion because of the need to exert tremendous amounts of energy trying
to survive in social contexts which are not conducive for Black men's survival. As Jamal noted, "you can only be frustrated for so long." Inevitably,
efforts to prove the negative images and expectations of Black men wrong
will lead to frustration when Black men constantly encounter life-denying
images of ourselves in spite of our efforts to live life free of such constraints.
This is part of what is unique about the care of Black men's mental health—
emotional healing must take place quickly for a Black man to be ready for
the next bullet of oppression that comes his way so that he can have an
opportunity to survive and thrive regardless of the realities of the social
pathology.[7]

NEGATIVE PROJECTIONS AND INTROJECTION

A Hope to Keep Going model of change takes seriously the process of
negative projections and introjection frequently occurring in the lives of
Black men. The processes of negative projections and introjection were highlighted in chapter four, along with their related dangers to the psyches of
Black men. Projection and introjection—named here as psychological processes guided by the workings of racism, sexism, classism, and heteronormativity in society—effectively work to keep Black men, and Black women, at
the bottom of society's social order. Caring for the mental health of Black
men necessarily means helping Black men resist the negative images and
expectations of Black men, and the ways that they are related to on a daily
basis, so that projected negativity is not severely introjected in the lives of
Black men. Despite the power of projection and the accompanying process of
introjection, Matthew stated that he "[w]ouldn't allow it to happen." In this
sense, Black men need a psychological disposition that will not allow the
negative projections of a racist, sexist, homophobic, and classist culture to
penetrate their psyches.

RESISTING NEGATIVE CULTURAL
PROJECTIONS AND INTROJECTION

The Psychological Task of Resisting Negative Cultural Projections and Introjection

In order for Black men to survive and flourish, they must resist negative images, expectations, and treatment of themselves in the media and society. Resisting negative cultural projection and introjection is essential to foster the survival, liberation, healing, and flourishing of Black men. The men in this book exhibited several ways to resist oppression amidst their daily experiences of being disregarded, disrespected, discredited, feared, and devalued. Their responses included: 1) meditating; 2) "proving them wrong" with positivity and intelligence; 3) "presenting other life options" for Black men; and 4) "cut[ting] people out" to alleviate psychological discomfort. These responses indicate that the Black men in this book are not passively accepting the negative images, expectations, and treatment of themselves in the media and society. Rather, they have developed ways to constructively and creatively respond to their social environments.

Lee Butler's Theory of African American Communal Identity Formation (TAACIF) provides a helpful way for understanding resistance. In his book, *Liberating Our Dignity, Saving Our Souls*, Butler proposes a new developmental theory, the Theory of African American Communal Identify Formation (TAACIF). Butler proposes that the lives of African Americans are developmentally experienced as two periods in life: 1) the *Foundational*; and 2) the *Constructive*.

> The first period suggests that the learning that takes place early in life and the issues that are confronted during those formative, foundational years remain as a permanent imprint upon the psyche. During the latter period of life, the individual continues to confront the foundational issues at a more profound level of functioning while she or he constructs a life with integrity, consistency, and wholeness. [8]

Butler's theory engages the historical reality of Black people in the United States as reference points and explains that Black people can respond to our realities with rage and creativity. In a personal correspondence, Butler stated that rage and creativity are two sides of the same coin. As such, the psyches of Black men can respond to feelings of hurt, woundedness, and sadness, and the accompanying feelings of frustration and anger with rage and creativity. Linked together, Black men's *rage* can be used as a resource to fuel our *creative* resistance against the presence of racism, sexism, classism, and homophobia in everyday life to survive and flourish. An essential element of Butler's theory of development toward the *Constructive* period of life is

African people's use of spirituality which has "energized African American creativity, making creativity a powerful adversary against the forces of hate and degradation."[9] In this sense, spiritual hope, as articulated in chapter five, must be viewed as an essential element of a Hope to Keep Going framework for care and counseling with Black men.

Reflection on Butler's TAACIF is critical for understanding and liberating Black male psyches from the devastating impacts of negative cultural images, expectations, and treatment aimed at Black men. Likewise, Butler's notion of *Learning the Rules* is vital to the constructive development of Black men. According to Butler's TAACIF, African Americans "learn the rules" of being Black in America during the first period of life. In the second period of life, African Americans learn how to "live the paradox" of life. It is, therefore, essential for those caring for the mental health of Black men to foster an adequate awareness within Black men of the need to "learn the rules" and to "live the paradox" of life as a Black person living in the United States of America and in the larger world.

CULTIVATING CREATIVE AND CONSTRUCTIVE AGENCY IN THE CONTEXT OF LIFE-GIVING COMMUNITY

Creative and constructive agency in Black men occurs only when it is, at some point, cultivated by members in the community where Black men develop and interact daily. That is, constructive agency cannot occur without a supportive community that cultivates ambitions within a person to use her or his own agency to effect positive change within self and the community. Gregory C. Ellison highlights the importance of a Community of Reliable Others to care for young African American men in his book *Cut Dead But Still Alive: Caring for African American Young Men.*[10] Similarly, a Hope to Keep Going model of change draws upon the resources of life-giving community to cultivate *self-reflection, self-awareness, self-regulation, motivation,* and *resilience* in Black men.

Figure 7.1 illustrates the Hope to Keep Going cycle of change that I have developed to nurture creative and constructive agency in Black men in the context of life-giving community. It holds that *self-reflection, self-awareness, self-regulation, motivation,* and *resilience* are critical for the psychological well-being of Black men. *Self-reflection* is the ability to reflect on the question: What is happening in my life? Experiencing healing and gaining direction for the future can emerge as one reflects on one's life. *Self-Awareness,* closely related to self-reflection, is a more in-depth and specific reflection on one's social placement in the world, the dangers one faces, along with the ways that one has participated in the world, including the outcomes of one's participation, and an honest assessment of one's strengths and weak-

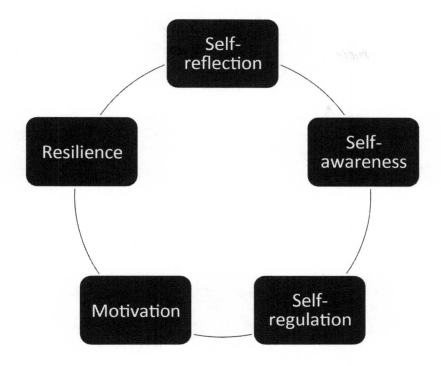

Figure 7.1. A Hope to Keep Going Individual Cycle of Change Diagram by Nicholas Grier

nesses. Understanding the theology and religious faith of others is also an important aspect of self-awareness. That is, due to the impact of society's religious commitment to the god of race and other forms of oppression, Black men must be aware of how totally rational people will invest their whole selves to the category of race and other forms of oppression. Black men must be aware of how totally rational people can commit the deepest parts of themselves to maintaining the status quo of racist, sexist, classist, and homophobic cultures, systems, and institutions. While totally rational people can think of themselves as committing themselves to what is right, they have actually committed themselves to the Demonic (when committing one's life to the perpetuation of racism, sexism, classism, and homophobia), which will always lead to destruction. Given this social reality, Black men must be aware of how all people in society are susceptible to maintaining a commitment to oppressive ideology and ways of relating. As a creative response, Black men must invest our total selves into a God, belief system, and/or ultimate reality which, in the Tillichian sense, is above and more powerful than the forces of oppression. Theologians have long acknowledged that if you control someone's god/God, you control their world. In this sense, Black men can develop increased opportunities for survival, liberation, healing, and flourishing when we: 1) acknowledge that totally rational people are controlled by the god of race (and, for our purposes, sexism, classism, and homophobia); and 2) invest our total selves to a God, belief system, and/or ultimate reality of liberation, healing, and justice. *Self-regulation,* defined here, is the ability to cope constructively with the negative images and expectations of oneself as a Black man, along with the negative ways that one is related to by society. It is in this realm that Black men can, following the lead of Lee Butler, respond to negative images and expectations of Black men with rage and creativity. Feelings of rage should not be viewed as pathological within themselves. Rather, if a Black man responds with rage,[11] the rage must be channeled creatively and constructively. Rage, in this sense, is a form of righteous indignation released and aimed at dismantling the injustices of the world. Amidst life-denying cultural environments, Black men must be *motivated* to pursue life-giving options for our lives despite negative images and expectations for our lives held by the media and society. Once Black men are motivated to survive and flourish amidst negative images, expectations, and treatment, Black men will inevitably experience moments in which they are knocked down by the workings of racism in American society. In order to resist being knocked down by negative blows to the self, Black men must develop and maintain *resilience* that enables us to keep getting back up to continue along our paths to survival, liberation, healing, and flourishing.

Having outlined the key tenets of a Hope to Keep Going cycle of change that nurtures creative and constructive agency in Black men in the context of life-giving community, it is important to acknowledge that communal and individual agency must work in tandem with one another. One without the other limits opportunities for the survival, liberation, healing, and flourishing of Black men. An embrace of a Hope to Keep Going framework for care and counseling means that communities and individual Black men work together to cultivate the survival, liberation, healing, and flourishing of Black men and women. An intentional embrace of creative and constructive communal and individual agency will cultivate a world of life-giving possibilities for the psychological survival, liberation, healing, and flourishing of Black men.

NOTES

1. Kohut identifies selfobjects as internalized external objects that one acquires throughout one's lifetime. Selfobjects can be people, culture, God, nontheistic religions, etc.

2. Phillis Sheppard, *Self, Culture, and Others in Womanist Practical Theology* (New York: Palgrave Macmillan, 2011), 113.

3. Sheppard, *Self, Culture, and Others in Womanist Practical Theology,* 115.

4. Sheppard, *Self, Culture, and Others in Womanist Practical Theology,* 42.

5. Sheppard, *Self, Culture, and Others in Womanist Practical Theology,* 45.

6. Positive psychology does this well by highlighting the positive dimensions of a person's psychological disposition.

7. This is not a "pull yourself up by your own boot straps argument." Rather, this is to say that as the community is working for the survival, liberation, healing, and flourishing of Black men, individual Black men can seek healing in a manner that enables us to be well amidst chronic experiences of individual, institutional, and cultural racism.

8. Lee Butler, Jr., *Liberating Our Dignity, Saving Our Souls: A New Theory of African American Identity Formation* (St. Louis: Chalice Press, 2006), 160.

9. Butler, Jr., *Liberating Our Dignity, Saving Our Souls,* 164.

10. Gregory C. Ellison, *Cut Dead But Still Alive: Caring for African American Young Men* (Nashville: Abingdon Press, 2013).

11. I am affirming that there are moments when rage is an appropriate response.

Conclusion

Journeying with the men in this book was a tremendous honor. I am forever grateful and indebted to them for the ways that they authentically shared their life experiences and perspectives. Similarly, I am thankful to the owners of the two barbershops who allowed me to connect with the men in this book. The presentation of their stories would not have been possible without the support of the barbershop owners and the men who participated in this project.

I initially set out to engage Black men on questions concerning the ways they have felt invisible, hyper-visible, and devalued. They resonated with the latter two. Yet, in an age so inundated with cases of police brutality against unarmed Black men, the men in this book demonstrated that they feel anything but invisible in contemporary American society. They stated that they feel very visible and expressed that they look forward to moments of being invisible, which, for them, means moments of peace.

CONCLUSIONS DRAWN FROM THE CONVERSATIONS

As previously mentioned, Lee Butler has named the importance of embodying a psychohistorical approach for theories and practices of pastoral care and counseling. In this sense, those caring for Black men should take seriously the lessons of history in the process of caring for the communal and intrapsychic experiences of Black men. A close study of history and the cultures in which Black men exist will aid pursuits to care optimally for the psychological well-being of Black men. Racism, sexism, classism, heteronormativity, and homophobia throughout history have negatively affected the identities and psyches of Black men. Therefore, theories and practices of spiritual care, counseling, and community leadership must wrestle deeply with the workings of racism, sexism, classism, heteronormativity, and homo-phobia and their impacts on the psychological well-being of Black men.

Negative images, expectations, and the treatment of Black men in the media and society often function as barriers preventing the survival, libera-tion, healing, and flourishing of Black men. Care for Black men, therefore, must engage the cultural realities affecting Black male communal and intra-psyhic experience. In addition to racism, sexism has negatively affected the identities of Black men to the degree that the men in this book demonstrated that they view manhood, in relation to women, primarily functioning through the roles of provider and protector, lacking empathy and support for the experiences and ambitions of women. This understanding of Black manhood must be engaged, critiqued, and dismantled.

This book also revealed that the psyches of Black men are quite active as they process their life experiences. They displayed common emotions of hurt, woundedness, and sadness, along with the accompanying emotions of frustration and anger. Communities, spiritual caregivers, and mental health therapists must work together to acknowledge and care for all of the emo-tional experiences of Black men comprehensively so that Black men will embody liberated identities and ways of relating that cultivate their flourish-ing and the flourishing of all in the global village, especially the vulnerable and oppressed.

CONVERSATION WITH GRANDMA SYLVIA

Much like the men in this book, my grandmother left a lasting impression on my life. Although she is deceased, I still remember her screeching voice singing in our small Atlanta church, along with a moment in my childhood when we walked together across the sanctuary after Sunday service to have a conversation with the church organist. In this moment, Grandma Sylvia ad-vocated on my behalf to make sure that I would have an opportunity to take piano lessons. The memory of the care she exhibited for my life lives on as a source of love and strength. The following is a fictive narrative I have created to capture the essence of what I imagine as her wisdom on the care of Black men in the twenty-first century that embodies a Hope to Keep Going frame-work for care and counseling.

Sitting downstairs on a couch in the family room in her urban Atlanta home, I engaged in conversation with Grandma Sylvia. Basking in her pres-ence, I re-encountered her stern yet caring presence that many of her grand-children had come to know and appreciate. I sought her wisdom: "Grandma, I want to free and heal America and the Black men living in this country. How can I do it? It seems there are so many obstacles to Black men living successful lives in America."

Grandma Sylvia responded in her scratchy voice, "Black men need a safe space to reflect. I was not perfect, and neither was our family. But one thing we gave you was a safe space to discover your own gifts and talents. We loved you and we believed in you. Black men need safe spaces where they can be affirmed and imagine themselves without the negative stuff about Black men in the media and society having the last word. The negativity about Black men is so hard to overcome. Negative images about Black men include portraying Black men as criminals and displaying them as people who can't be in caring and empathic relationships with Black women. This has to change. And it all starts with the family."

"Yes. But," I interjected, "surely our family was not perfect."

"Correct. One of the things we could have done better was listen to you more deeply. I suppose we could have listened more deeply to your own ambitions, passions, and your experiences of struggle and hurt. In a similar way, Black men need to listen more deeply and empathically to the experiences of Black women."

"True," I continued. "We need to re-imagine Black manhood so that Black men exude greater empathy and offer more support for the experiences and ambitions of Black women. Yet, aren't we missing a key point and being naïve about all Black men having family support? Not all Black men will have loving families."

"Maybe not blood families," she declared. "But this doesn't mean that the community can't be a loving and supportive extended family for Black men."

"Well, that makes sense," I responded. "I've heard people declaring that we need Black men to embrace extended fatherhood and take seriously the adoption of other young Black men.[1] And what if the community, such as schools, barbershops, faith communities, counseling centers, politicians, and policy-makers made spaces to listen and care for the emotional experiences of Black men so that we can survive and flourish while simultaneously deconstructing patriarchal, sexist, homophobic, and classist ideology? Wouldn't that help change the cultures in which Black men exist? Ah, and one more idea: What if part of our efforts for care included transforming the music and film industries so that the media communicates messages that foster the psychological flourishing of Black men and women?"

With an affirming smile on her face, she responded, "Now you're thinking." On that note, she returned to her rest.

NOTE

1. Here I am referring to the works of Lee Butler, Jr. (2010) and Michael Cook (2014).

Appendix A

Vignettes

VIGNETTE #1:

Quinton is a bearded, Black man in his mid-thirties. A bandage loosely covers a large wound on his left hand. The vignette below is from a visit with Quinton on a sunny November afternoon on the South Side of Chicago at a public clinic that services individuals living with infectious viruses. The clinic employs doctors, social workers, pastoral counselors, case managers, and nurses to care for the holistic needs of patients. My job was to care for patients' emotional and spiritual health. The protocol was such that when the medical doctor knocked on the door, she or he had the right to enter the room and my session with the patient would end as long as the session was at a place where we could quickly conclude without the patient feeling emotionally overexposed and overwhelmed. However, I established a healthy rapport with the medical doctors so that if I needed more time to finish a session with a patient, they would respect my request and give us a few more minutes to conclude.

When I first met Quinton, he felt emotionally guarded (understandably so, given his experience in the world as a Black man) and often said "I'm good, I'm good" when I asked him how he was doing. However, on this particular day, after I entered the room, I noticed that even though he didn't say much, something was different about his mood. He seemed more subdued, as if something was on his mind. I followed my hunch and attempted to nurture a space where he could feel supported and comfortable enough to open up about whatever was on his mind.

By the description of many, Quinton would be considered a gang-banger and well-versed in South Side of Chicago street culture. A Hope to Keep Going framework for care and counseling taps into the rich resources within

Quentin and his community in order to tend to his grief and imagine a hopeful present and future.

Therapist: Hi, Quinton. Good to see you today. How are you? (Several seconds of silence pass. I notice his mood is slightly different today—a little more somber.)

Quinton: I'm good. (Many of the men in the clinic started off giving this type of response.)

Therapist: What's going on?

Quinton: (A few seconds of silence pass.) My cousin James was murdered by a gang a couple days ago.

Therapist: Aw, man. So sorry to hear.

Quinton: We grew up together. We grew up playing together in the projects.[1] I can't believe he's gone.

Therapist: Yeah. That's tough.

Quinton: I wish I could have protected him and done more for him. (Seconds of silence pass.) I admired the way he lived, though. I'm gonna miss him.

Therapist: I can imagine. It sounds like you all were really close.

Quinton: Yeah. He meant a lot to me. (Silence passes.) All this is making me think a lot. I think about why him and not me. (Silence passes.) But yeah, it's tough. I want to live my life to honor James.

Therapist: I feel you. That makes sense. How can you live your life to honor James?

Quinton: I don't know. He was just so positive about everything and knew how to laugh and have a good time. You would never know that we didn't have no money comin' up because he was just always so positive about everything.

Therapist: It seems like James knew how to keep things in perspective and have joy no matter what was happening in his life.

Quinton: Yeah. I don't know how he did it.

Therapist: How do you think he did it?

Quinton: I think he just had something inside of him that knew it was more to life than life on the streets and gang life.

Therapist: It seems like he had great perspective. You mentioned that you want your life to honor your relationship with James. Do you think you can use some of what you've learned from James' life and apply it to your life?

Quinton: (Some silence passes) Yeah. Definitely. It's like he never let anything really get to him. He just lived his life.

Therapist: That's powerful. He was determined to live the way that he wanted to live no matter how difficult the circumstances may have looked around him.

Quinton: Definitely.

Therapist: That determination is important, especially as a Black man. You know, I'm thinking of how important it is for Black men to be determined to make it and thrive in life, regardless of the circumstances. Maybe you can use this moment of reflecting on James' life to adopt some of his strengths to overcome whatever struggle you might face in your life.

Quinton: Yeah. I can see that. How are you thinking?

Therapist: Well, I'm thinking about the struggle that can be part of living life as a Black man. You've had to be resilient growing up in the projects and, even now, fighting this virus. I think that you can use the example of James' life to reflect on your own life and to have inspiration to do and become whatever you want to be in the world. And in the process, I'm certainly here to support you.

Quinton: I really appreciate it. Yeah. This whole death of my cousin hit me real hard. It came out of nowhere.

Therapist: I can imagine.

Quinton: But I see what you're saying. It's tough that he ain't here no more (tears up . . . a few seconds of silence pass), but I know I can honor his life by living my best life.

Therapist: I think so. I'm willing to be here with you as you process it all.

Quinton: I appreciate it.

I present this vignette to illustrate a case in which the most pressing concern is "survival," as identified in figure 6.1. Quinton is trying to survive every day as a low-income Black male with a challenging health condition. The community must work with him to help him resist self-defeatist thoughts and practices and to resist oppressive institutions, cultures, and relationships, which do not acknowledge his full humanity. Quinton is also experiencing grief. The "healing" phase of the communal model of change (also identified in figure 6.1) must be engaged at this point in Quinton's life. In the midst of his grief, I invited Quinton to "self-reflect" (as identified in figure 7.1) as a way to work through his grieving process and appreciate his relationship with his deceased cousin. As he self-reflects, he will be able to gain greater self-awareness of the blessing of his cousin in his life. He might also gain self-awareness of the ways that he can strengthen bonds with other men in his life, like his cousin, who can help him resist oppression. A community of "life-giving brothers"[2] can function as a resource to nurture his survival, liberation, healing, and flourishing.

VIGNETTE #2:

Brandon is a Black man in his late twenties. I first saw Brandon at a counseling center in downtown Chicago for a counseling session with his girlfriend, Simone, who requested that they go to therapy to work through their relationship difficulties. After a few conflicts arose during their couples counseling sessions, I agreed to see each of them for individual breakout counseling sessions in addition to their couples counseling sessions. Brandon stated that he grew up with uncles engaging in polygamous relationships. However, his girlfriend did not agree with polygamous relationships and was significantly hurt because Brandon continued to engage in romantic and sexual relationships with other women during their relationship. While she didn't like Brandon being involved with other women, she continued to give him another chance. It appeared that she was more invested in the relationship than Brandon, although Brandon's vision of the relationship was a polygamous one while Simone maintained visions of a monogamous relationship.

Brandon was typically late to our counseling sessions and the vignette below continued this trend. He was about ten minutes late to this counseling session.

Therapist: Hi, Brandon. Good to see you. I'm glad we found a chance to connect. How are you?

Brandon: Yeah. Fa sho. I'm glad I could make it. They had me working all types of crazy shifts, but I definitely wanted to make our time cuz I know we set it up and I want to be a man of my word.

Therapist: Well, I'm glad you made it. How is work coming along for you?

Brandon: It's aight. It's taking care of the bills right now, so I can't complain.

Therapist: That makes sense. How are you doing overall?

Brandon: Well, I've been thinking a lot about our last session with Simone. I love her, but it's just hard for me to settle down with one woman because my uncles always had more than one woman. So it's hard for me to imagine having a monogamous relationship with her.

Therapist: I see. Can you say more about how your uncles thought about relationships with women?

Brandon: Yeah, well they always said, "Brandon, you know you have options and you can have more than one woman at a time." So, I just grew up always feeling that was the norm. Being with Simone is making me have to be something else, and I don't know how to be that type of guy. I don't know how to be satisfied in a monogamous relationship.

Therapist: I appreciate your honesty. So, essentially, the way you think about relationships with women comes from your uncles.

Brandon: Yeah, definitely. That's all I saw growing up.

Therapist: That makes sense. We often repeat what we see before we critically think about how we want to live. Now that you are older, what do you think about the examples your uncles left before you as it relates to relationships with women?

Brandon: I can definitely see how it might hurt a woman, especially if she doesn't want to be in a polygamous relationship. But, at the same time, that's all I knew growing up, and it's hard for me to imagine being something else.

Therapist: I see. Can you say more about why it's hard to imagine being something else? And I imagine by something else you mean being in a monogamous relationship?

Brandon: Yeah. Fa sho. And that's a good question. I think it's just cuz I never saw anything else in front of me.

Therapist: That's real. One of the things that can be difficult as we grow into the person we want to become is differentiating ourselves from the connection with people we love and the things that the people we love believe. But I think it's possible to love the people in our lives—whether it's family, close friends, or other people—and still choose how we want to be as adults.

Brandon: I see what you're saying.

Therapist: You said you can see how the ways that your uncles treated women can be hurtful to women, particularly a woman like Simone who wants to be in a monogamous relationship with you

Brandon: Yeah.

Therapist: During our couples counseling sessions with Simone, we've seen her hurt and cry because she felt you weren't faithful to her.

Brandon: True. But some of it is her insecurities and I told her that I struggle with monogamous relationships.

Therapist: I understand. However, I want to pull from the strength of what you said. You said that you can see how your uncles' approach to relationships with women could be hurtful. It seems as if you might be replicating that same way of relating to women. It seems to me that you can also think about how Simone feels when you are talking to other women. While she might have insecurities, it's important to think about how she feels and how she experiences you. If you aren't able to be in a committed monogamous relationship with her, do you think it is fair to her?

Brandon: (Brandon shifts his body in the chair.) I guess not. (Brandon seems to have an ah-ha moment. A few seconds of silence follows.) I think it's best that we break up. I can't be in a monogamous relationship right now and I don't want to hurt her more than I already have.

Therapist: Hmm. That is a significant revelation. I think it's important for you to be thoughtful and very caring with her if you decide that you no longer want to be in the relationship. It won't be easy and it will be important to care for her in the midst of the process. But I'm glad that you have a little more clarity on where you are in your life right now and that in order to not cause any more hurt to Simone, it's best to discontinue the relationship. It's important to think about the feelings of women and to show that we, as men, are genuinely concerned with how they feel.

Brandon: Yeah. Thank you. (The session ends and Brandon shakes my hand firmly before he leaves. This was our last session as he did not return for therapy after this session).

I present this vignette to illustrate that the process of change towards a liberated Black male identity can be a slow process. Referencing figure 7.1, I worked with Brandon in the "self-reflection" phase of the cycle. It would take his community, family, and perhaps another therapist to help Brandon wrestle deeply with the insights that come from his self-reflection so that he can move towards greater self-awareness, self-regulation, motivation, and resilience, particularly in the area of rejecting and resisting oppressive patriarchal norms so that he can cultivate empathic and supportive life-giving relationships with women.

VIGNETTE #3:

Kevin is a Black man in his mid-thirties who is flourishing. He has worked in the banking business since graduating from a local Chicago university. The task in this vignette is to help him reflect on his life experiences and help him experience emotional healing amidst the constant need to reject negative images, expectations, and treatment of Black men in society and in his professional life.

Therapist: How are you, sir?

Kevin: I'm well. Glad to be off of work (chuckles). How are you?

Therapist: I'm good. It's been a busy season, but I am enjoying it.

Kevin: That's good. It's always good to enjoy the work that we do.

Therapist: Indeed. You mentioned being glad that you're off work. How are things coming along at work?

Kevin: Things are going well. But since we've been having our conversations, I've been thinking more about how hard I've had to work as a Black man in these environments. I realize that I've been working hard and working to resist all of the negative images and expectations of me as a Black man since the day I graduated from college and began my professional career. I've done well, but it is exhausting. I've become more aware of the ways people just naturally look right past me or don't social-ize with me as a Black man on the job. As I mentioned, I'm grateful that I've been able to have success, but our conversations have helped me to tap more into the emotional toll it has on my mind and body to keep trying to portray this almost perfect image of myself as a Black man on the job.

Therapist: That sounds tough.

Kevin: Well, I always try to represent to the best of my ability every positive aspect of what a Black man should be as much as possible.

Therapist: I can see that in you. Why do you think it's important to always represent the best of what a Black man should be at every mo-ment?

Kevin: It's important because so many people in corporate America, and I guess America in general, have stereotypes of a Black man. They might see us as lazy, not intelligent, and a threat. That's not how everyone sees us, but in my experience in corporate America, there are a lot of people who see Black men that way. My line of work, the banking industry, can be so racist. And I'm like, "Do you see me?"

Therapist: When you ask yourself if they see you, what is your response?

Kevin: Well, you have to think about not only the great and influential African Americans who've done great things throughout history, but also there are so many Black people doing great things. Yes, you have Presi-dent Obama, but it's not just Obama. There are so many Black people doing great things in many different areas. The media just doesn't show it. So I see the negative images of Black men, but I also know my self-worth.

Therapist: Where do you get your positive sense of self-worth?

Kevin: Growing up at Bethany Methodist Church, we were always taught to be proud of our Blackness. So, I've got a lot of cognitive dissonance with the ways they try to treat me at work. In those moments I recall that I am unashamedly Black and unapologetically Christian. There's freedom as a Black man in embracing that type of thinking.

Therapist: That's powerful. It sounds to me like throughout your life and career—in spite of the obstacles—you've been able to survive and flour-ish.

Kevin: Yeah, but it's not easy. It takes time and work. It takes being committed to always refusing to give in to the negative stereotypes and expectations society has of Black men.

Therapist: Do you ever get tired? By this I mean, do you ever get tired of always trying to be the best version of a Black man and needing to make your mark?

Kevin: Well, that's a good question. I don't think I've ever really stopped to think about that question. Since college, I've had to prove myself on the job and have become accustomed to doing whatever it takes to get the job done.

Therapist: That makes sense. I've felt similarly in my life. As you look back on your work experiences, do you think always having to represent positive aspects of a Black man and working to leave your mark is the best approach? In other words, I'm wondering if there is a way for you to have at least a moment of relief when you don't feel the pressure to always be the best version of what a Black man should be.

Kevin: You know, I never really thought about it that way (a few seconds of silence pass), but as I think about it, I can see it being helpful to have a routine where I reflect on my experiences as a Black man and use those moments to heal my emotional wounds. Thank you for bringing that up.

Therapist: What do you think it will be like to acknowledge and heal your emotional wounds?

Kevin: (chuckles) That would be great. Your questions are helping me think about my past and present experiences that I hadn't really thought about in this way. It feels good to talk through these experiences. Hopefully these types of conversations can be helpful for me and many other people.

Therapist: Well, I hope so. Yet, as I think about our conversation, it seems that you are already flourishing. So, it's important to acknowledge the great parts of yourself that have enabled you to push through barriers and become a successful Black man. You should really be commended for the strength and vision you've maintained throughout your journey. I'm also glad to hear that this conversation has been helpful for you to constructively reflect on experiences from your past and present. In order to help you continue to flourish, and go deeper in your flourishing, it can be helpful for you to reflect more on your experiences as a Black man and to make space to tend to your own emotional healing.

Kevin: I think you're right. I must say that I am looking forward to continuing these types of conversations. Our reflections are different than the normal types of conversations a person has during the day and it's very helpful.

Therapist: I'm glad. Well, you have a very good ability to self-reflect and have great gifts to help other Black men survive and thrive.

Kevin: Well, thank you for all of this. It has been excellent. Looking forward to connecting next time.

Therapist: Sounds good. Take care of yourself.

I present this vignette as an example of the work that can be done with a Black male who is flourishing. While Kevin is in the "flourishing" phase of figure 6.1, he needs a therapist, spiritual caregiver, and the community to work with him to "continuously become woke" of the ways that he might be exerting extra emotional energy always giving 110 percent to prove wrong the negative images and expectations that the media and society have of Black men. A therapist, spiritual caregiver, and the community can work with him to ensure that he has moments to rest, reflect, tend to his emotional wounds, and live fully into his authentic Black self as he flourishes.

NOTES

1. By "projects," Quinton is referring to low-income housing.
2. By "life-giving brothers," I mean Black men who are concerned with the well-being of other Black men. Any Black man can be a life-giving brother to another Black man, regardless of whether or not they are biologically related.

Appendix B

Individual Interview Questions

Black Male Identity & Hyper-Visibility

1. What does it mean to be a Black man?
2. Describe the images of Black men that you see in today's media.
3. What does U.S. society say about Black men?
4. How do you deal with images of Black men in the media and U.S. society?

Invisibility

1. What does it mean when a person is treated as if he's invisible?
2. Tell me about a time in your life when you felt invisible.
3. What do you do when you feel invisible?

Male & Female Identity

1. What does it mean to be a man?
2. What does it mean to be a woman?

Devaluation

1. What does it mean when a person is devalued?
2. Tell me about a time in your life when you felt devalued.
3. What do you do when you feel devalued?

Faith & Spirituality

1. What does hope mean to you?
2. Does something give you hope in life? Is so, can you tell me about it?
3. What does spirituality mean to you?
4. Has spirituality been helpful in your life? If so, can you tell me about it?

Appendix C

Research Participants

All names presented here are pseudonymous to protect the confidentiality of research participants.

Participant: Matthew
Ethnicity of Biological Parents—Mother: Caribbean Father: Dominican
Birth City: Chicago
Age: 36
Highest Degree Earned: High School Diploma
Annual Income: 50K–75K
Profession: Entrepreneur

Participant: Kendrick
Ethnicity of Biological Parents—Mother: Black (from Barbados) Father: Black (from Chicago)
Birth City: Chicago
Age: 36
Highest Degree Earned: B.S. Degree
Annual Income: 50K–75K
Profession: Telecommunications

Participant: Darrell
Ethnicity of Biological Parents—Mother: African American Father: African American
Birth City: Detroit
Age: 29
Highest Degree Earned: B.S. Degree
Annual Income: Not known
Profession: Entrepreneur

Participant: Eddie
Ethnicity of Biological Parents—Mother: Black Father: Black
Birth City: Chicago
Age: 26
Highest Degree Earned: B.A. Degree
Annual Income: None
Profession: Graduate Student

Participant: Jamal
Ethnicity of Biological Parent—Mother: Black Father: Black
Birth City: Chicago
Age: 25
Highest Degree Earned: High School Diploma
Annual Income: 21K–34K
Profession: Barber

References

Anderson, Victor. *Beyond Ontological Blackness: An Essay on African American Religious and Cultural Criticism*. New York: The Continuum Publishing Company, 1995.

Baldwin, James. *Notes of a Native Son*. Boston: Beacon Press, 1955.

Belgrave, Faye Z., and Kevin W. Allison. *African American Psychology: From Africa to America*. Thousand Oaks, CA: Sage Publications, 2019.

Bell, Derrick. *Faces at the Bottom of the Well: The Permanence of Racism*. New York: Basic Books, 1992.

———. *Silent Covenants: Brown v. Board of Education and the Unfulfilled Hopes for Racial Reform*. New York: Oxford University Press, 2004.

Bell-Jordan, Katrina. *Masculinity in the Black Imagination*. Edited by Ronald Jackson and Mark Hopson. New York: Peter Lang, 2011.

Buber, Martin. *I and Thou*. New York: Scribner, 1958.

Butler Jr., Lee. *Liberating Our Dignity, Saving Our Souls: A New Theory of African American Identity Formation*. St. Louis: Chalice Press, 2006.

———. *Listen My Son: Wisdom to Help African American Fathers*. Nashville: Abingdon Press, 2010.

Charmaz, Kathy. *Constructing Grounded Theory*. Second Edition. Los Angeles: Sage Publications, 2014.

Cook, Michael. *Black Fatherhood, Adoption, and Theology: A Contextual Analysis and Response*. New York: Peter Lang, 2014.

Du Bois, W. E. B. *The Souls of Black Folk*. New York: Barnes & Noble Classics, 1903.

Ellison, Gregory. *Cut Dead But Still Alive: Caring for African American Young Men*. Nashville: Abingdon Press, 2013.

Fanon, Frantz. *Black Skin, White Masks*. New York: Grove Press, 1952.

Gehrie, Mark. *Progress in Self Psychology: Basic Ideas Reconsidered*. Edited by Arnold Goldberg. Vol. 12. Abingdon: Routledge, 1996.

Griffin, Horace. *Their Own Receive Them Not: African American Lesbians and Gays in Black Churches*. Eugene, OR: Wipf and Stock, 2010.

Harris, Angela, and Emma Jordan. *Economic Justice: Race, Gender, Identity and Economics*. New York: Foundation Press, 2005.

Head, John. *Standing in the Shadows: Understanding and Overcoming Depression in Black Men*. New York: Broadway Books, 2004.

hooks, bell. *We Real Cool: Black Men and Masculinity*. New York: Routledge, 2004.

Jeffries IV, William, Brian Dodge, and Theo G. M. Sandfort. "Religion and Spirituality among Bisexual Black Men in the USA." *Culture, Health & Sexuality* 10, no. 5 (June, 2008).

Johnson, Cedric. *Race, Religion, and Resilience in the Neoliberal Age*. New York: Palgrave Macmillan, 2016.

Kohut, Heinz. *How Does Analysis Cure?* Chicago: The University of Chicago Press, 1984.

Lartey, Emmanuel. *In Living Color: An Intercultural Approach to Pastoral Care and Counseling*. Second Edition. London: Jessica Kingsley, 2003.

———. *Postcolonizing God: An African Practical Theology*. London: SCM Press, 2013.

Lewis-McCoy, R. L'Heureux. *Hyper Sexual, Hyper Masculine? Gender, Race and Sexuality in the Identities of Contemporary Black Men*. Edited by Brittany Slatton and Kamesha Spates. New York: Routledge, 2016.

Marable, Manning. *Race, Reform, and Rebellion: The Second Reconstruction and Beyond in Black American, 1945–2006*. Third Edition. Jackson: University Press of Mississippi, 2007.

McWilliams, Nancy. *Psychoanalytic Diagnosis: Understanding Personality Structure in the Clinical Process*. Second Edition. New York: The Guilford Press, 2011.

Namageyo-Funa, Apophia, Jessica Mullenburg, and Mark Wilson. "The Role of Religion and Spirituality in Coping with Type 2 Diabetes: A Qualitative Study among Black Men." *Journal of Religion & Health* 54, no. 1 (2015).

Parker, Evelyn. *Trouble Don't Last Always: Emancipatory Hope among African American Adolescents*. Cleveland: The Pilgrim Press, 2003.

Pinn, Anthony B. *Terror and Triumph: The Nature of Black Religion*. Minneapolis: Fortress Press, 2003.

Ray, Stephen. "An Unintended Conversation Partner: Tillich's Account of the Demonic and Critical Race Theory." *International Yearbook for Tillich Research* 9, no. 1 (2014).

Shelby, Tommie. *We Who Are Dark: The Philosophical Foundations of Black Solidarity*. Cambridge, MA: The Belknap Press of Harvard University Press, 2005.

Sheppard, Phillis. *Self, Culture, and Others in Womanist Practical Theology*. New York: Palgrave Macmillan, 2011.

Shorter-Gooden, Kumea. "Therapy with African American Men and Women." *Handbook of African American Psychology*. Edited by Helen Neville, Brendesha Tynes, and Shawn Utsey. Thousand Oaks, CA: Sage Publications, 2009.

Smith, Archie. *Navigating the Deep River: Spirituality in African American Families*. Cleveland: United Church Press, 1997.

Stolorow, Robert. *The Intersubjective Perspective*. Edited by Robert Stolorow, George Atwood, and Bernard Brandchaft. Northvale, NJ: Jason Aronson, 1994.

Tillich, Paul. *Biblical Religion and the Search for Ultimate Reality*. Chicago: The University of Chicago Press, 1955.

Walker-Barnes, Chanequa. *Too Heavy a Yoke: Black Women and the Burden of Strength*. Eugene, OR: Cascade Books, 2014.

Wallace, Michele. *Black Macho and the Myth of the Superwoman*. New York: Verso, 1999.

Ward, Jesmyn. *Men We Reaped: A Memoir*. New York: Bloomsbury, 2013.

Watkins, Daphne, Rheeda Walker, and Derek Griffith. "A Meta-Study of Black Male Mental Health and Well-Being." *Journal of Black Psychology* 36, no. 3 (December 2009).

Watkins Jr., Tommie L., Cathy Simpson, Stacey S. Cofield, Susan Davies, Connie Kohler, and Stuart Usdan. "The Relationship of Religiosity, Spirituality, Substance Abuse, and Depression among Black Men Who Have Sex with Men (MSM)." *Journal of Religion & Health* 55, no. 1 (2016).

Watkins Ali, Carroll. *Survival and Liberation: Pastoral Theology in African American Context*. St. Louis: Chalice Press, 1999.

Williams, Patricia. *The Alchemy of Race and Rights: Diary of a Law Professor*. Cambridge, MA: Harvard University Press, 1991.

Wright, Almeda. *The Spiritual Lives of Young African Americans*. New York: Oxford University Press, 2017.

Wright, Richard. *Black Boy*. New York: Harper Brothers, 1945.

———. *Native Son*. New York: Harper & Row, 1940.

Index

About the Author

Nicholas Grier, PhD, LPC, is assistant professor of practical theology, spiritual care, and counseling at Claremont School of Theology (Claremont, CA). He is also a counselor at The Clinebell Institute and founder of Coloring Mental Health Collective, a community-focused organization that advocates and organizes for the mental health of Black and Brown people.